THE
The Journey Within & The Rise From Defeat
HIGHER
YOU

LOAY RAGHEB

Copyright © 2009 Loay Ragheb
All rights reserved.

ISBN: 1-4392-3991-6
ISBN-13: 9781439239919

Visit www.booksurge.com to order additional copies.

I would like to dedicate this humble work to my incredible parents, Fadel and Higar. My father taught me to take risks and he always believed in me, even at my lowest point. My mother was always there when I lost my way and needed a place to hide from the world.

To my son, Fadel, you are the candle that shines my darkest moment.

To my partner I am grateful for the patience and endless support.

To my editor, David Bernardi, thank you for helping me communicate my vision.

To my masters & generous teachers Prophet Moses, Prophet Jesus, & Prophet Mohammad Peace & Prayers Upon them, I would like to say thank you for your struggles and your unwavering strength before evil.

I would like to humbly offer my ultimate thanks, gratitude, and endless praise to my creator, who through the difficulties He put me through, helped me rise as a man, a human, and gave me endless gifts of humility and inner joy, and I ask Him with a kneeling head to forgive me for all my shortcomings, transgressions, ill deeds, and to shower me with the gift of forgiveness.

AMEN

Contents

Preface vii

Introduction xi

PART 1: THE FIVE MASTERIES 17
Chapter 1: Tame Your Internal Beasts 21
Chapter 2: Asceticism 49
Chapter 3: Water-Based Living 63
Chapter 4: Build Inner Wealth 71
Chapter 5: The Path to Sage-hood 77

PART 2: LESSONS FROM THE PAST 87
Chapter 6: The Apple 91
Chapter 7: Seek Beauty 97
Chapter 8: The Bird 105
Chapter 9: Seek Knowledge and Act 111
Chapter 10: The Mosquito 131

PART 3: PURIFY YOUR HEART 137
Chapter 11: Conditions of the Heart 139

THE 20 SYRUPS OF REFLECTION 169
Conclusion 175

Preface

In January 1991, my plane touched down at Montreal airport. My cousin Yusuf back in Charlotte, North Carolina, where I went to school, had warned me of the cold weather in Canada. He said, "If you're standing out in the cold waiting for a ride and the ride is fifteen minutes late, you will freeze to death." He was joking of course, but I took him seriously.

The laughter my family greeted me with still echoes in my ears today as I exited the airport gate wearing at least three jackets and two pairs of pants.

While that was funny, the circumstances that forced me to come to Canada were sad. The war in Kuwait had forced us to immigrate to Canada seeking a new beginning. We faced many difficult days as we adjusted to our new home. We opened and operated a small restaurant while I finished school. After graduation, I joined one of Canada's top Investment firm as an advisor, working solely on commission during my training period. I also worked weekends and during the week at the restaurant to sustain a reasonable level of cash flow.

Upper management placed bets that I would fail within the first few months. The fact is, I had no contacts, no extended family, I didn't know the city, and I didn't even speak the French language. Nevertheless, I was able to break everyone's expectations and become one of the top advisors at the firm year after year. I built a solid team of roughly sixteen advisors, managing millions of dollars for Canadian families. My income surpassed the $400,000-per-year threshold, and life was sweet. The field was very difficult and demanding despite its financial rewards. I have earned every dollar for the endless late nights, weekends, and lost dinners at home being on the road and at clients' kitchen tables. The responsibility of managing clients' money came with a heavy price: I was ignoring my inner needs as a human being, and the bigger picture behind my existance.

Nevertheless, I was living the American dream, as they say. I bought a brand new home, a sports car, and I simply had fun spending like a madman. But despite all the pleasures of the senses, the *inner void* was always present. Soon enough, I was subject to betrayal at work, and I began to spiral downward, losing my home, my family, my business, and my money.

This was the first of series of discoveries that I made. My eyes had opened to the cruelty of life and the brutality of the human race. My void had now come to surface, and I discovered that what I had was nothing more than a mirage. This happened to me in the year 2000, eight years before the collapse of the global financial system in 2009. While the world was flourishing, I had lost everything I built, and the world had turned a blind eye to me.

Today, eight years later, I have emerged stronger, wiser, and determined to pursue what truly matters in life. I looked around and began to see masses of people scrambling to make sense of what is happening while I remained calm and collected. My own disaster happened long ago, and my recovery took its time while the world was on autopilot. Through this journey of eight years, I have read more than five hundred books and explored every avenue to understand the source of my inner pain. I was the unluckiest man alive only to emerge with a smile in the breeze of life. I have discovered what matters in life, what makes us whole, what gives us inner peace, and what gives us the strength to be what we wish to be. Most of all, I discovered that becoming wealthy is truly nothing more than mastering the richness of the inner self.

To this day, I face struggles between the material, external world and the inner world of serenity and peace. I have discovered that these struggles never truly end, but they can cease to exist for as long as I decide. Sage-hood is the ability to stand in the face of an earthquake of external ruin while remaining fully intact on the inside. This power is priceless.

—Loay Ragheb

Introduction

When my journey towards awakening began, a thought came to mind. If you took a man and placed him in a cell, locked the cell and placed it underground, and supplied him with enough water, food, and air to survive, would the power of manifestation, or the power of some mystical "secret," ever help him? The truth is many men did die in small cells lost in some underground prison, where no dreams or wishes are able to save them. There is no law or secret or great hidden power that can bring such men to the surface.

As I pondered this problem, I came to one incredible answer. For any of our desires to manifest in reality, two things must happen: one, you must possess the freedom to act, and two, you must *act*. While this may not seem like an incredible revelation, it led to a most incredible discovery ever for me. I realized that the ultimate secret is not to manifest the big home, the expensive car, or all the riches of the world. The greatest achievement is the mastery of your ***inner world***.

This mastery can free you from all your physical and mental prisons, lifting you from darkness into the light. Every secret about the manifestation of greatness exists in the fertile soil of the deep inner self. This explains the monumental contentment that men like Jesus, Mosses, and Muhammad (peace be upon them), as well as the sages of the East, were capable of.

The whole world is extremely focused on building external wealth, and this focus has led to a collective imprisonment of the human race. I discovered through my own experience that creating wealth on the external side of our existence is simple; creating internal wealth is much more demanding. During my highest financial point and my lowest, I always had an inner void and a pulse of pain that never went away until I was able to awaken to true inner mastery—even if only for a few moments a day. The only difference between when I was broke and when I had money was that the blinders on my eyes seemed thicker when there was financial abundance, and that I was better at ignoring my inner pain. However, until I achieved true inner mastery, the pain was always there, a sharp inner pain emanating from the void within.

Many around you have begun to experience this deep void. Look around you, wherever you go. Look at the anger, the confusion, the self-destruction, the fights, the broken relations, the loneliness, the bankruptcies, and the masses suffering deep inner pains. We have been running in a maze of material attachment for so long that we have long since forgotten the priceless inner treasures we need in order to be whole and healthy. The information in this book will help you rise above the impoverished state by building a foundation of inner wealth. This information will help carry you through the most difficult times in life, and if you are fresh in life, it will provide you with the needed ammunition when your test arrives.

This book defines success at a deeper level, igniting the dormant forces for change we are all born with. It addresses the physical and the metaphysical, the two dimensions that every human must heed to be happy and content. I aim to come to you from every possible direction, using stories, theoretical models, thought-provoking concepts, prophetic wisdom, and religious concepts to help you overcome adversity, both internal and external.

In bringing the information forward, I draw on a variety of sources. I will use wisdom from the East and the West, stories that happened thousands of years ago and as recently as when this book was written. You will find teachings from Jesus, Moses, Mohammad, Peace Be Upon Them, and other men who travelled the earth spreading incredible jewels of wisdom. You will also be presented with psychological analysis, poetic prose for the artist in you, wise conversations for the deep thinker, as well as my own personal experiences—provocative ideas that will make you think. While many of the stories derive from religious texts, I wish to emphasize that the goal of this book is not to endorse any set of religious beliefs—or religious belief in general—but rather to open your heart and mind to the forces of change.

You might read one story and be inspired beyond belief, or you may read a provocative thought that triggers instant awakening inside you. You may come across a quote that opens your heart and mind to inner change or pushes you to do something you have never done before. Passages from this book might be completely irrelevant to you today but come in handy in the future. If you promise yourself to read until the very end, you will have accomplished something important. Your inner magnet will pluck from these pages ideas that it's been screaming for all along.

Overcome the evil forces within you and rise. Allow these pages to help you. Happiness is no more than small increments of growth, internally and externally.

"You must triumph over your inner oblivious state of mind. By doing so, you will stimulate your heedful self. Your heedful self will deliver you to a higher stage in life and into inner peace." —LR

The Beginning of Your Slavery

We live in a world filled with pain, personal disasters, greed, confusion, and blindness. While all these negatives exist, love, peace, harmony, health, success, riches, power, and a joyful life exist as well. Unfortunately, when searching for the tools necessary for achieving a powerful, successful life, many of us resort to chemicals such as alcohol, antidepressants, anti-anxiety and anti-psychotic pills, as well as natural feel-good "drugs" such as excessive food and material objects to ease the pain.

Every scientific or psychological breakthrough begins with a question that reflects our need to know. You and I use the word "why" many times on a daily basis, whether out loud or to ourselves. In order to solve the complex problems in our lives, we first "feel a need" for something and then figure out what it will take to accomplish what we seek to solve.

The needs that arise in us are part of the process of finding our inner path. When you feel angry, sad, or happy, you are experiencing a state resulting from the interaction with your environment. These feelings compel us to act in certain ways, many of them destructive. This means that feelings should be monitored, controlled, and understood in order for us live a balanced, peaceful existence.

The first step towards awakening is turning your focus inwards with an observing inner eye that recognizes the triggers of depression. When we fail to do this, our needs control us, and we allow our inner *autopilot* take control. From this point, it isn't long until we find ourselves in a completely **hijacked** state.

Science explains depression as an imbalance in the chemicals our brain produces, leading to symptoms such as persistent feelings of hopelessness, dejection, poor concentration, lack of energy, inability to sleep, and sometimes suicidal tendencies. When we lack the mastery to control our inner world of feelings and reactions, tremendous pressure is exerted on our brains, and as we age, the brain begins to malfunction and our world moves from a healthy existence to a chaotic one. Like any part of our body, the brain then begins to fail as a response to the constant pressure.

Throughout our life, we are subjected to a continuous stream of events. We are exposed to duties, surprises, societal law, religious law, moral law, relationship dynamics, needs, desires, disappointments, successes, failures, chaos, danger, disaster, illness, and pain. These factors induce a reaction in your physical body, and if you are not awakened to these inner reactions (in the form of feelings), your body becomes fatigued, and that fatigue is expressed through anxiety, depression, and more. Unless you completely eliminate all your external and internal stressors, you are on the path to malfunction, a state of illness and unbalance.

We train our bodies in the gym to build muscle and improve cardiovascular ability to cope with pressure, improve the overall health of the body, and shed unwanted fat. If you don't exercise at all, consuming large quantities of food and sitting down for long hours, you will experience a variety of ills, not to mention difficulty breathing at the slightest physical activity. Just as the body needs to moderate consumption and engage in activity to maintain functioning, the brain requires training as well, but the type of training the brain needs is quite different. Rather than intense training, what the brain needs is rest.

When the brain is under stress, it produces a chemical response. For example, if you are under financial pressure, you will feel fear (of becoming homeless, for example), and that fear causes the body to enter fight-or-flight mode, triggering the release of harmful chemicals. Knowing it must moderate this fear, the brain pumps other hormones and chemicals, which the blood absorbs to induce a state of calm. A vicious cycle ensues, causing an inner imbalance in the form of pressure, anxiety, delusions, low energy, fatigue, irritability, and an overall feeling of guilt and sadness. At this stage, people resort to the fastest, most readily available solutions to these inner disturbances—drugs (prescription or otherwise), excessive eating, drinking, smoking, and other pleasure-producing indulgences.

This process is largely unconscious, and our inner world becomes subject to a hijacked state, a continuous stream of inner disturbances and fatigue resulting from dealing with external stressors. We must begin to look at these feelings as **controllable entities**. We must realize that *what you feel* is not *who you are*, but merely a reaction to an external event, a perceived threat or need.

Your Inner Autopilot/
The Hijacked State

Many of our basic needs are magnified and manipulated by the impulse for extra joy, the lust for more pleasure. For example, we must eat because the body needs a certain amount of food for survival. We must eat for nutrition and strength daily; however, anything above our basic biological need becomes an indulgence, and regular indulgences eventually become a destructive habit. This is the result of an internal battle between the desire to feel immediate pleasure and the desire to feel and look healthy. Soon, this entire process becomes unconscious, manifesting in the *autopilot state*, in which we no longer even consider the question of whether to overeat or not. The most appropriate state to describe overweight individuals is that they are "out of control." They are committing the act of putting the food into their mouth, but they are not mindful of this act. They have let their inner autopilot act for them.

Why do we easily say "I have no control" when it comes to chocolate, rice, pizza, and other pleasurable foods? The answer is *association* and *heedlessness*.

Association is a method the autopilot state uses to induce the state of "loss of control." We associate food with pleasure, and our brain understands it as an antidepressant, providing relief from a depressed mental state resulting from external problems we are facing. The result is that one set of feelings and desires overcomes another opposing set of feelings of restraint.

The dilemma is that most of us are living in a state of *heedlessness*, in which we are completely unaware of our autopilot condition. In our formative years, we went through these inner battles of the feelings over and over again:

- Should I eat a second dish, or should I not eat a second dish?
- Shall I drink the whole bottle, or shall I not drink the whole bottle?
- Should I go to the gym or watch television?
- Should I wallow in self-pity in the face of bad news, or shall I focus on the good?

At a certain stage, and after a number of years in a state of heedlessness, we eventually become completely hijacked by a set of feelings and desires, forcing us to live as a prisoner to a destructive internal design. When we order a pizza, we finish the whole thing instead of having a couple of slices, and when presented with the opportunity, we cheat on our partner. We have given up being awake and present when these internal battles arise. Our current character is the result of many years of inner decisions. The result is a sleeping state, in which you are *completely hijacked*. In fact, these inner forces, desires, or feelings have more than hijacked you; they have enslaved you. By giving them power over their opposing positive impulses, you have given them the mandate to sway you, control you, and direct you.

Feelings are powerful, and the more you feed them to satisfy certain desires, the more enslaved you become to those desires. It's like a fire that you keep throwing logs of wood into. But eventually the fire will burn out: picture yourself constantly borrowing to feed your shopping desires until you are unable to resist or restrain yourself! This will only lead to your financial disaster.

Smoking for twenty years is another example—the smoker will have consumed more than fifty thousand cigarettes on average, and the craving never ceases! Likewise, the drinker, the overeater, and even the rage-aholic seeks to establish a state of normalcy, yet continues to feed his inner beasts. These beasts eventually usurp his main role as king of his inner domain and the conscious controller of his internal battles. This is when the *hijacked self* takes hold.

Are you a slave or a master?

In addition to being a slave to our impulses, many of us are slaves to the system that allows us to feed these impulses. Take a reflective look at your daily actions and describe your day. Look at everything you do, say, and feel. Are you truly involved in the decision-making process, or are you present only in smaller, non-essential matters? Can you for a moment reflect on the power the dollar has over you?

Allow me to ask you the following questions. In an average week,

- How many hours do you spend working for a living?
- How many hours do you spend thinking about work?
- How many hours do you spend worrying about the future?
- How many hours do you spend worrying about the debt you have accumulated to satisfy material feelings of instant gratification and ego-based desires?

Why do you think tycoons who come face to face with huge losses end up slitting their wrists or jumping in front of moving trains? It is because they have become complete slaves to the material possessions they accumulate, in some cases even becoming crooks to satisfy their endless feeling of inadequacy when they compare themselves to richer men or women. The void inside of each of them has never been satisfied with material accumulation. All you ever satisfy with wealth is physical pleasures and bodily comforts. Some this insatiable state can be overcome by giving to charities, the poor, or family. They seek to fill the inner void through good deeds. While it is a great thing to do, the void shall never be filled through riches alone or giving alone. Emancipation from the slavery of the material world is what's required.

"The one constant, never-changing element of material possession is that it either passes on to another or vanishes when you die." —LR

* * *

The void is present in each of us to some extent. The void grows slowly with every wrong decision we make and with every triumph of our lower self. However, the control mechanism to overcoming this dilemma is also present in each of us. Inside your universe, many forces are either working harmoniously or are in a state of conflict. The same is true when describing your external universe.

This book will look at ways to shut down your inner autopilot and overcome this hijacked state by turning the eye inward, at the inner world. Part 1, "The Five Masteries," will teach you the essential techniques for knowing your inner world and bringing harmony to it. Part 2, "Lessons from the Past," shares collected wisdom from the ages in the form of parables that shine a divine light on the inner world. Part 3, "Purify Your Heart," is a roadmap to cleansing your inner world of the ego-based detritus it accumulates as it drifts through life and achieving true sage-hood.

PART 1: THE FIVE MASTERIES

The journey toward your deep inner self is beginning. We are simply a manifestation of all that lurks within us. You have internal demons and enemies that you must confront. The sooner you come to accept the need to wage this battle, the sooner you will be on your way to full recovery. Full recovery means a life of bliss, inner harmony, and a progressive material existence. Wealth without peace is like land without rain. You must emerge victorious, allowing the rain of wisdom to descend on your inner fertile land. In order to achieve this peace, one must become a student of the five masteries.

In chapter 1, I will introduce the most ferocious inner beasts that you must bring under control. With this awareness, you can then apply the same techniques to all other inner beasts.

Chapter 2 concerns the mastery over the five senses, otherwise known as *asceticism*, a crucial step towards a stronger, more resilient you. This is the difficult part, and I am a firm believer in achieving this mastery over time and, most importantly, with patience. What was built over years should be rebuilt with a plan, and you must take protective measures to minimize the shock to your world.

When the mastery over the senses begins to manifest through action, a new approach towards life follows. I humbly suggest the incorporation of *water-based living* at this stage in your daily life. This approach will aid you in overcoming difficulties, resistance, frustrations, stress, and impediments to success. This is the subject of chapter 3.

In chapter 4, we will discuss the healing of the internal wound called the *inner void*. This healing will require a new approach towards the material world. Again, while I am an active participant in the material world, I also value freedom. Freedom from the slavery of the materialistic system can happen either acquiring an abundance of material positions or by detaching oneself from the fabricated desires of the materialistic system; through the latter means, we begin to subdue our inner imbalance. I will address how you can become the master of wealth rather than a slave of wealth. As you begin reflecting on all facets of your life, you will take another step on your journey toward completeness.

The fifth mastery, discussed in chapter 5, is the ascending process through the stages to sage-hood. This mastery is never permanent or easily accomplished. However, even for a glimpse of sage-hood, the effort is absolutely worth it. In the few days I was able to experience this stage, all resistance melted, people flocked towards me, trees spoke softly, and I felt unstrapped by anything. This stage comes and goes, and the mastery of permanent sage-hood is a bliss very few achieve. I am content for now to experience it every now and then.

> **"When inner awakening begins, the soul will always seek it, like an infant seeking the face of his mother."**
> **—LR**

* * *

Chapter 1: Tame Your Internal Beasts

"Inside every man lurks beasts of destruction that, if allowed to surface, would destroy his life." —LR

While growing up, you made an endless amount of decisions. Your life today is the result of those numerous decisions. If you examine your life closely, you will begin to understand the state of heedlessness you exist in. You are no longer the captain of your ship, and you are definitely not the judge residing on your own inner supreme court. You currently part human and part machine.

Inside you exists the mechanism of **opposites**. When you wish to do something, a message is triggered—a thought in response to your inner intention. The intention is what decides the outcome, or the act, that follows. For example, you are at a family gathering, and you have a drink with dinner. You wish to have another, but an inner voice says, "You must be careful. If the police catch you on the way back, you could get into great trouble." Then another voice responds, "Come on. It's only one more drink. I am okay. I can handle this." The moment you decided to have the second drink, you have empowered that second set of thoughts, which responded to your voice of reason. As time passes, the initial voice of reason begins to shy away, and the **autopilot** is engaged.

This applies to every facet of your life—your relationships, your financial affairs, your eating habits, and so on. In time, a large number of autopilots are operating at once, resulting in a fully **hijacked state**. Have you noticed how so many pedestrians simply begin walking when the light turns red, not even bothering to see whether the cars have come to a complete stop? This state of heedlessness is the result of blind trust that has developed due to multiple experiences safely crossing the street. The reality is all it takes is one instance of a car failing to stop for injury or death to result. People often trust their very lives to a set of autopilot systems, not realizing how they are being controlled.

The first step toward awakening is to shed light on your decision-making process in every facet of your life. For you to become heedful again, you must open your internal eyes and ear to observe and listen to your internal dialogue whenever it takes place.

Listening to your internal dialogue is the beginning of awakening. It is the path through which you can reclaim your life. Every step you take is a step that will lead either to your demise or to your resurrection. Success in life depends on this initial step.

***

Awakening from your hijacked state

To begin to heal from the state of heedlessness, you must simply make the decision to become *involved* again. Becoming involved means listening to your inner conversation. Start to listen whenever you are about to make any decision. Awakening begins with the simplest, most basic decisions. Even the way you take your coffee can be a great starting point. Every time you order or make a coffee, bring your full self into the experience and allow no external distractions stop you from focusing on the process. How many spoons of sugar do you take? How much cream do you put in your coffee? When I was going through a very tough diet to lose the extra twenty-five pounds I was carrying around, I began to pay attention to these details. While I listened to the voices appealing to my pleasure centres, which told me to add sugar and cream, I decided to heed the voice that said I must reduce my sugar and cream intake. I decided that to begin, I would slowly reduce sugar and cream, allowing myself the occasional indulgence.

Time passed, I reduced my cream intake, and it was not long before I stopped putting sugar in altogether. This was only possible by bringing my attention to the process, allowing myself the room to fail and to indulge at times. Today, I cannot even stand sugar in my coffee, finding that it actually destroyed the taste of the coffee.

While this is not a book about diets, it is a book about awakening. Simple things in life can lead you to bigger awakenings. The process of showering in the morning was always about waking up and getting my body clean. I would get into the shower and find myself done before I knew it. It just became a habit. More than five years ago, I decided to actually *enjoy* my showers, fully immersing myself in the experience. While my shower time never changed, lasting roughly ten minutes, those ten minutes began to feel like an eternity. Why? Because I was present in the experience, thinking about nothing but the water and the sensations, shutting the door in the face of all other worldly thoughts.

* * *

Be mindful of the present

Time is the one commodity worth experiencing. We often fail to see that our life is not the objective we desire but also the moments leading up to that objective. We seek riches to achieve a state of constant happiness and to escape the pain of time. Little do we know that this pinnacle, or place, called *happiness* is constantly moving forward, yet we endlessly spend most of our moments in its pursuit. I will not say that happiness is here and now, because when you have debts, job loss, marriage breakdowns, and other pressures, you are not going to be all that happy, but you must understand that there will always be something you are unhappy about. That "place of complete contentment" is a mirage; it can never exist on the outside. It can only reside within you.

To awaken from the deep inner sleep of the autopilot self, you must come back to the present moment and invest in it. Take reading this book, for example. Are you in a rush to finish it in order to find all you need, in order to use the knowledge within to achieve your desired result? If you are, you are missing the golden chance to fully *live* the experience of the book and to fully comprehend the concepts being presented. I am here with you in this moment, and we are intertwined on this journey of discovery. You must live the experience of the book one statement at a time and one concept at a time. Using your imagination, your inner visual aids, your thought processes, and your internal wise eye, you will understand even the words I failed to write and the ideas I failed to uncover.

Once you begin to bring the attention to your inner conversation, you begin to reclaim your world. You become a true master of your actions, and in turn influence your surroundings a great deal. Wealth, as I said, is a matter of inner self mastery that will manifest in your external world if you desire and worthy of the blessings. Pain is the result of an inner autopilot, which your own mind has created as a normal response to a particular material loss, such as the loss of money, job, spouse, or possessions. You have decided on the amount of pain that is appropriate in most situations. The exception is the pain of loss when a loved one passes. This pain will reflect your true inner strength, but your tears may also provide a means of washing away deep-lurking stress-related illnesses. The death of our parents is what makes us truly capable of facing the rest of our short lives.

A tale of mindfulness

A woman went to check on her ailing infant as she cared for him for a few days. There was no doctor in the village, as this took place more than thirteen hundred and forty years ago. To her shock, she discovered that her baby had died from the fever. She sat beside him and cried softly for an hour, and then she washed him and wrapped him in perfumed white garments. She then placed him in his crib and pushed the crib behind the door away from the eye of any who came into the home. Hurriedly, she cleaned the house until it was spotless, took a long bath, donned the best of her garments, applied makeup to her face, and waited for her husband. Her husband arrived and asked kindly for dinner to regain his strength after working in the fields all day. She brought him the best food she could muster, and they sat talking and laughing. He asked about his little infant boy, and she said, "He is in complete rest and in the finest of states." He smiled and decided to check on him in the morning. They went to bed shortly after, and they made love that night.

The next morning, after breakfast, she broke the news to her husband. He was engulfed in anger and broke into tears. Why she didn't tell him the night before, he asked, and she explained, she knew how tired he was coming home from a full day of work in the fields, and hearing such news in the darkness of the night would multiply his agony and cause him ripping grief.

The husband, still angry, went to speak to the wisest man in the village, complaining about the actions of his wife and seeking his advice. The wise man smiled and said, "Did she meet you with full makeup?" The husband replied yes. "Did you sleep with her last night?" The man answered yes. The wise man said, "You have a gift in this amazing woman. She not only spared you the pain of the news in the darkness of night; she also bore the heavy sadness on her own all night long, and slept with you to instil in you the hope of having another child. All that she did was to ease your pain." The wise man was the prophet of Islam Muhammad Peace Be upon Him.

* * *

"Every female represents a kingdom of love, giving, care, beauty, intelligence, abundance, and affluence. That's why it is crucial that a female seek the love of the man that can penetrate her outer physical shell and be able to see the kingdom of beauty within her. A woman's exterior beauty can be manipulated by diets, surgery, cosmetics, exercise, and makeup, but her interior beauty, when mastered, and her inner strength, when sharpened, will make her priceless." —LR

* * *

A great reward of awakening from the hijacked mind is the ability to choose a partner based on their inner beauty and strength. This awakened choice can elevate you to a higher status, allowing you to shine rather than face the destruction that comes with pursuing false relationships based on physical attraction.

Conversation with a monk

Over a thousand years ago, a virtuous man asked a monk for a piece of wisdom. The monk said, "Wisdom is to be in a state similar to the state of a man who is surrounded by beasts and viscous animals—he scared, aware, and alert. He knows that should he fall into heedlessness, then these beasts would rip him apart; if he forgets their presence, they will attack him from every angle. Be in a similar state as this man, and you will posses wisdom."

The virtuous man said, "Tell me more, monk."

The monk said, "The thirsty would quench his thirst with a few drops of water."

When the pious man contemplated the advice of the monk, he understood that what the monk meant: Each of us must become awakened to the internal beasts we carry. Each of us who looks deep within, with the light of wisdom and attention, realizes that he is filled with viscous internal beasts: anger, jealousy, arrogance, vanity, hate, unquenchable desires, greed, gluttony, and more. Each of these beasts can rip us apart from the inside if we are to ignore their presence.

Many are unaware of these inner beasts, yet once the inner veil is lifted, we can see our inner beasts with clarity. They are the snakes and scorpions that that continuously bite us, and these bites are ill actions we do through our daily life. If we are to overcome the inner snakes and scorpions, we must do so before they reach our heart, the deepest spot of our inner self, and bite us there. Most of the people you hear about on the news, the people who destroy their lives, are in fact victims to their own hijacked mind and to their inability to shed light on the true enemy that lurks within.

The feelings described above are normal human feelings that we all experience from time to time, but when they appear regularly, to an extent that you begin to notice an inner state of confusion and lack of productive energy, you must understand that your inner beasts are at work and your body is sending you messages to awaken. The greatest disaster is when people seek medical attention, in the form of chemicals, to correct the problem. These do little more than silence your inner voice of reason, which is crying out for a constructive, deep remedy.

Instead of pausing, reflecting, and deciding to change your inner and external world by healing and awakening, you impose an extra layer of heedlessness, giving the beasts within you the ability to work with complete secrecy and without interruption. Sooner or later, you have to stop taking these chemicals, or your body will no longer respond to them, or perhaps something in you will be triggered that will cause you to commit an irrational and most likely destructive act.

The solution to manifesting your inner harmony starts with awakening from the state of heedlessness described above. Then, you must face your inner beasts by recognizing and naming them. The most destructive beasts come in the form of arrogance, greed, and materialism. Let's shine a light on each of these beasts to see how they affect your life and how to overcome them.

Arrogance

This inner beast has the tenacity and strength of a thousand wild horses. With its devious ways, arrogance gives us a false sense of self-worth. We are all humans with worth, rights, and uniqueness. We are all a celebration of life. Yet arrogance leads you, its victim, to believe that you are above everyone else, and that your worth is greater than that of others. Arrogance is responsible for the demise of thousands of great men and women around the world.

Recently, I responded to a classified ad from an agency looking for unique voices for radio and show business. I had been on the radio a few times, and I thought to myself, "Why shouldn't I call? It wouldn't hurt to get an assessment, even if it costs $20 dollars. It would be great fun," I thought to myself.

I asked my wife to come, and we went on our way. When we got there, we were greeted by two ladies with the warmest, most sincere smiles and attention. We were lead to room full of chairs in what appeared to be a seminar room. One of the ladies handed us a sheet of paper with five paragraphs to read—copy for commercials or short news articles. Our task was to speak these lines aloud in the recording studio. Inside the studio, we were greeted by a gentleman, most likely a manager, with warmth and great attention. As I stepped into the studio and started recording, the man showered me with warm compliments and encouraging words. Further, he stressed my talent and the uniqueness of my voice. I stepped out and waited for the final assessment, which I learned would take place next day at 1:00 p.m., via phone call. The two ladies thanked us with an immense amount of warmth and attention. We then went home.

The whole thing was to convince me to sign up for a $4,000 course, which would prepare me for a career in radio. I declined respectfully despite the praise I received on my voice. However, the experience got me thinking about Hollywood and the lengths people will go to achieve fame. I caught a glimpse of what actors and actresses go through on a daily basis. The attention they get is incredible. I imagined receiving the attention I got in that recording studio, increased at least tenfold, and getting such praise every day. I would surely become an addict. Actors and actresses often face this shocking dilemma when the lights shy away from them. When actors are abandoned by their close circle, they often go through a shock. These professional "companions" are shrewd and know how to play on the ego and arrogance of others.

The attention we seek is the result of our ego's deep hunger for self-worth and importance. When this attention suddenly vanishes, we experience a level of pain relative to the amount of attention we used to get. Arrogance is a product of internal and external factors that fool you and me into believing that we are special, or above others. Our prejudices, our racist thoughts, and our need to judge and stereotype people all spring from our arrogance. This does not suggest we are all equal in our levels of education, manners, success, kindness, wisdom, intellect, cleanliness, talents, or abilities. On the contrary, there are vast differences in these areas, and we all seek to improve our status through knowledge, wisdom, education, financial success, and more. Arrogance however, leads you to believe that you are incomparable, irreplaceable, unshakable, and an incredibly special human being. Because of these beliefs, we engage in reckless behaviours such as overspending, acquiring what we think we need to improve our value in the eyes of others (advertising executives are specialists in playing to people's arrogant notions of self-worth). Interestingly, the approval we are seeking is through the eyes of those who share the same ego-driven goals.

Words have the power of magic. If you allow your inner beast of arrogance to take hold of you, you become weak and easily manipulated in the presence of sweet tongues. Facing your arrogance is a very difficult battle. We are humans and we seek confirmation from our surroundings and others. This is why so many men and women flock to take pictures with celebrities and hang them on their wall. These celebrities do not even know them, but in their mind, they feel special to have shared a moment with them, believing it will gain them instant credibility in the eyes of others.

* * *

Arrogance also explains why many people are willing to pay $2,000 a ticket to be part of a dinner reception with a well-known figure, and it can lead others to believe that they "deserve" a better spouse, career, or social standing. These people fail to see the blessings they have in their life, always on the lookout for something better. This leads to a tormented state of being.

Do not misread this as an excuse not to seek more from life. On the contrary, I am stating that arrogance can blind you to the great riches that exist in your life right now. I am sure you know that health is not a right, but a privilege. Have you ever experienced a large knot in one of your shoulders? Imagine if this knot would not go away, only grew as your tension increased. Your life would be crippled and unbearable.

*　*　*

A wise man in the presence of a king was asked about true wealth. As the king awaited the answer, the wise man slowly smiled. He asked the king to drink five large glasses of water and the secret would be revealed. The king abided and began drinking.

When finished, he said to the wise man, "Nothing happened, oh wise man."

The wise man asked the king to wait for a few moments. A few moments passed, and the king stood up, excusing himself.

The wise man said, "Where are you going, oh great king?"

The king replied, "To the washroom, oh wise man. Your suggestion must be emptied now with a smile."

The wise man smiled and said, "Do you understand now, oh great king?"

"No, I don't know what you mean," the king replied.

The wise man then said, "If I gave you a choice, great king, the gold of all the seven kingdoms or the ability to go to the washroom right now, which would you choose?"

The king smiled while shaking his head, and said, "To go to the washroom, wise man."

*　*　*

Naturally, you and I look at the story and appreciate its humour. However, we rarely fully immerse ourselves in the wisdom it teaches us. We tend to appreciate only the gifts we have taken for granted when we lose them.

Begin an honest discussion with your inner self and understand that the only true praise comes from within, not from the outside, and that your inner praise should serve your ability to be humble in the face of the world.

The first step to taming the beast of arrogance is *self-reflection*. **Ask yourself, "What have I offered humanity? And what has humanity offered me?"** This placement of the self in the proper context tends to bring me down to earth. Have you invented a product that made life easier for your fellow man? Are you the discoverer of insulin or aspirin? Have you invented the car, the plane, the light bulb, the map for the human brain, paper, ink, the mobile phone, asphalt, tires, cranes, trains, and so forth? The answer to this question may help you appreciate the status of great men and women, those from all over the world who have worked exceptionally hard to advance our life and give us the enormous comforts we enjoy today.

The second step to cleansing your inner world from the illness of arrogance is the ***awareness of death***. Yes death, for no great man or woman ever lived forever. Death can come to you at any moment, through a virus unseen by the naked eye or the cheapest of weapons. When you regularly remember death, you are regularly remembering your place and your true value.

The third whip to tame the beast of arrogance is **knowledge**. When you seek and acquire knowledge, you become aware of how little of it you truly have. Standing before the mountain of knowledge, you can observe your small size. Standing atop the mountain, you see the vast, infinite range of mountains left to climb. The achievement of taming the beast of arrogance will make you a stronger human being. As the tale above demonstrates, no king or queen was above the natural laws of life. Men of great power were overtaken by the people, including the great pharaohs of Egypt and the most vicious dictators of the modern world. Hitler, who was on the brink of taking over the world ended up taking his own life with a bullet worth less than twenty-five cents.

* * *

..............................In the Torah and the Quran, the story of Moses and Pharaoh proves that if a man does not humble himself, the days will sure humble him. The cycle of life points to the eradication of arrogance. The aging process offers continual and ever-increasing reminders that you are not as powerful as you may think and that each and every moment of your life is truly a special gift that never comes back again.

The secret worth sharing with you is that once your arrogance disappears, your worldly success begins to appear. The world is designed to reward those who, despite the knowledge they have of their true weakness, keep on marching towards greatness.

Greed

"Greed is the castle of agony." —LR

We are designed to consume what we need to sustain our daily living. Jesus noted this long ago, asking his Lord to give him his daily bread, which was enough to sustain him. While we are not living in biblical times or the desert of Arabia, where men like Abraham and Mohammad (peace be upon them) dwelled, we can still heed the lessons about the human race these wise men left us.

Greed is the means by which the void seeks to relieve its pains. The desire inside you will never die. It has no intellect or abilities except to satisfy its goal. You must be heedful and alert in order to recognize this aspect of your life and control it.

The stock market is a place where fortunes are made and lost. Many invest in hopes of building sufficient funds to retire successfully. As a financial planner, my job is to help others plan for the future, build wealth, and accomplish their financial goals. After meeting with more than four thousand Canadian families over my fifteen years of experience in the field, I have had the golden opportunity to observe different characters and human conditions. Greed was always the main ingredient of unhappiness. I remember one client who had over $2,000,000 invested with me. She was seventy-eight at the time. She had a simple dream, and that was to drive a Jaguar. I remember that at each meeting we had, she would mention it, and I would repeatedly say that she should buy it. However, nothing would convince her. While childhood issues clearly affected her, the fear she had didn't stop her from pursuing the $3,000,000 mark. Was she greedy, or was she crippled with fear? The two go hand in hand. Greed creates fear, and fear creates greed. At the end, she died before achieving her lifelong goal of driving a Jaguar.

Steve, on the other hand, was a thirty-seven-year-old successful doctor. I remember meeting him a while back as we went through his financial planning process. When we were done, he looked at me and said that the portfolio I had suggested was too conservative for him, and that he wished to take higher risks to achieve a higher rate of return. I tried to explain that he had accumulated a respectable amount and that his monthly savings would naturally make him a millionaire before age fifty. He dismissed my plan and in fact went with a big downtown firm that he thought would fulfill his desire. Steve invested over $400,000 in one investment, sold through an offering memorandum in a start-up oil Company. The firm administering the investment, placed the client's assets in the Bank of Montreal, and borrowed against the capital a multiple amount to the placed guarantee. The market crashed, the Bank of Montreal called in the loan, and the investment collapsed. Arrogance and greed resulted in a substantial setback in Steve's financial status. Why? Greed is at the heart of the decision to amass wealth quickly. This highly paid professional could have continued with a balanced approach, arriving at his destination safe and sound.

Greed can cloud your judgment and subvert your moral code. Greed also leads to debt, a tyranny that most of us have suffered at least one time in our life. We want to drive the best cars, put on the best clothes, travel, go out, have fun, live in big houses, and much more. One should not deny oneself the pleasures of life, but greed should never be a factor in achieving one's goals. Rather, we should master our skills, be faithful in our field, and that will eventually make us rich. Greed is truly a disease, yet, as the old saying goes, "contentment is a fortune that never evaporates."

* * *

To simplify, awakening is a combination of essential tools to establish harmony in one's life. If you give rule only to intellect, life will have no taste to it and you will live like a machine. If the heart alone rules, you will have a kingdom from the dark ages, and if your desires lead to a mutiny you will be on the path to destruction.

Greed is a failure to be awake at every juncture and during every decision. To begin to curb greed, you must invest the time to write down your true desires and objectives in life. You are not meant only to work and accumulate money. Likewise, you are not designed to seek constant sexual fulfilment with multiple partners, and you are not designed to eat your way to the grave.

There is a secret behind pleasures: unless they are pursued properly, the risks are great. I didn't design the system, and nor did you. I didn't design the human body, which dictates that if you sleep with multiple partners, you may contract a fatal STD. For reasons beyond our choosing, indulgence comes with a risk that can be fatal. You must understand this lesson to lead a balanced life.

Greed is a beast of brutal consequences. They can cause you to lose yourself to a set of desires that you mistakenly think life is all about. You have five senses, and while each requires a certain amount of attention, you should be a slave to none of them. Slavery comes in many forms, and if you examine your life closely, you will begin to recognize the types of slavery you are currently experiencing. To overcome the slavery of the senses, I have designed a sample solution, which will be discussed in the following chapter.

***

Materialism

I am a financial strategist and investment advisor by trade. My professional life has been a constant exposure to wealth building. Money can make life far more bearable. The power to do what you want whenever you want is fascinating. We are always seeking this freedom through wealth. While wealth is a positive source, it can also become a nightmare. Our obsession with wealth and the luxuries of life often induce internal stresses that manifest in agitation and lack of patience.

While greed is seeking more of a good thing, materialism is judging everything—including oneself—according to the level of wealth one amasses. Greed corrupts the mind, the body, and the soul, and materialism corrupts our relations and results in a weak and false life. A materialistic individual seems to judge everything around him or her based on wealth. Think of driving in the morning and seeing another person pass you with a luxury car. Notice your internal dialogue. Do you instantly have respect for him, or envy him, or instantly assume that he is wealthy and worry free? Many seem to judge others according to their material possessions. In my short life, I have come across men and women dressed to the teeth, wealthy, and exceptionally good looking but who lacked the intellect to engage in a conversation beyond their vanity and material possessions. I felt suffocated talking to them. They lack deep reflections, life-based conversations, analysis, or even the skill to talk about important human concerns. To them, money was the answer to everything, and through the wealth they had amassed, they felt that they had become somebody.

This is a phenomenon of our culture. We are bombarded daily by commercials and TV shows and movies that weaken us spiritually. We seem not to recognize our greatness and worth unless we can express it in material terms. This does not mean that a successful person is always vain and empty, but financial success does not mean a man is deeply valuable from within. Wealth cannot buy you a true sense of contentment.

We live in a culture that is focused on one thing and one thing only, and that is consumption and the creation of wealth. This may sound strange coming from a financial advisor, but it is true. Our daily obsession with financial matters and objectives leads to an unhealthy view of life. Endless hours are lost either seeking wealth or thinking about it. To add to the dilemma, our need for instant gratification often arises due to the capitalist society in which we live. We see wealth around us daily and we want a piece of the action to satisfy our hunger.

The daily friction with the material world often subjects our internal being to prolonged periods of sleep. This can be referred to as the "spiritual coma." It becomes increasingly difficult to turn on our inner joys, because as the years pass, we identify joy simply in relation to external factors. A hijacked mind feeds on its materialistic environment.

Our senses relate the external material world to us, via touching, smelling, feeling, seeing, and hearing. You need no spiritual awakening to taste food or enjoy sex; however, your pleasures will be heightened and more satisfying if you experience them while you are awakened. We often eat fast foods, communicate in terse, to-the-point sentences with each other, and even interact sexually with our spouses at an animalistic level. We rarely take the time to fully enjoy the pleasures derived from external daily activities. Multimillionaires indulge in daily pleasures oblivious to their true essence, and so do the poor and the middle class. Perhaps you have heard of the fisherman in the village who was encouraged by a friend to start a fishing company. The fisherman asked why he should do that. His friend explained that by succeeding in business, he could have a lot of money. The fisherman replied, "And what do I need so much money for?"

To which his friend said, "To fish and have a good time."

The fisherman said, "But I am fishing and having a good time now."

Many do not know a fundamental rule when it comes to wealth creation. This rule is hidden in the answer to two major questions:

- What is your true reason behind seeking wealth?
- What are you willing to give up achieving wealth?

When you answer the first question you must be careful. Most around you would say things like:

- I want to buy a bigger home.
- I want to travel.
- I want to provide my children with an excellent education.
- I want to buy the best clothes.
- I want security in a shrinking economy.
- I want to play more golf/sail.
- To buy my dream car and a summer cottage.

While this may not be your particular list, most people's answers are similar. I had the privilege of interviewing thousands of clients asking them this question. I wish to reveal a secret to you that great men and women figured out a long time ago. **To achieve great deeds and amass wealth, you must follow a noble cause.** This noble cause must serve the human race. The objective should always be beyond your own selfish needs. If your financial objectives are always focused on your own personal needs (including those of your immediate family), you will always be amongst the ranks of the average people.

If you look around, no billionaire has achieved wealth without providing a service to the human race—period. Think about the following question carefully; if you answer correctly, you are easily on your way to the land of riches.

What can I do to serve the human race?

Eliminate your own needs from the equation for once, and your heart will provide you with a unique answer tailored to your own unique capabilities. The answer will change your life. Learning to overcome selfishness and exchanging self service with the service of others will not only revolutionize you life but will take you to a higher state of awakening experienced by few men and women around the world.

Men like Jesus, Mohammad, and Moses (peace be upon them), regardless of whether you believe in their message, have built the largest institutions in the world. Jesus has more than 2.8 billion followers, Mohammad more than 1.3 billion, and Moses more than 20 million. These men came with a message designed to serve mankind. Examine for a second the ills mankind has committed with these messages and you will find the root is in selfishness and earthly desires.

When you learn to apply the rules of the service of others, you will uncover the manifestations of your own greatness. Many great men died without a nickel to their names and had no wealth from the material world. However, they possessed an eternal abundance within. They faced difficulties and abuse on the hands of the people yet emerged victorious, immortalized in our consciousness.

The answer to this question defines the quality of life you will lead. When the material world blinds you, you become a slave to time management, balancing systems, and stress-coping mechanisms. You are to choose the things you are willing to give to attract more of the material world. At times, a long conversation with your child or regular bonding with true friends can be worth more than what earth can provide you. I am not suggesting that you become a prophet or an entity of detachment from the material world.

I am suggesting that you observe the priorities of your life in order to choose wisely.

One thing I want you to take from this is to look with an eye to the future. I have come to notice the loneliness in people's lives as they age in our western world. I have seen men and women living alone at old age, with rarely anyone knocking on their doors. The question you must ask yourself is, "Will the money I have dedicated my life to offer me any solace when I am older and alone?" I have seen women cry before my eyes from loneliness and fear of dying alone, men barely capable of walking yet living alone. I don't hold the answer to this problem except to say that we need to invest more in our children and our relationships. We cannot expect to dedicate our life to financial gain while ignoring our relationships. I have seen brothers and sister who speak once a year, or haven't heard from each other for ages. I have seen parents eager to send their children out the door, and in turn their children rush them into retirement homes. We exchange love with money and true friendship with an extra suit to wear. It is absolutely horrific how lonely people are in our land. We as a society have some sort of dislike or fear of old people. I have never figured it out. Could it be because they remind us of the true weakness of the human condition? Could it be because we do not want to be associated with the old? How can we go from loving our parents to sending them to die in a retirement home? They die and we seem to have missed building memories with them. We seek to have fewer children, making the excuse that life is too difficult. Is it truly difficult, or do we wish to have more for ourselves? If you have a major heart attack that would leave you half paralyzed, alone, and with no friends or children to care for you, was it worth it?

* * *

If you walk away from this book with this one lesson—that you should invest more in relationships as opposed to financial greed—you have truly saved your future life. Reflecting on this can help you see what is truly important. If you have a brother, have a regular ritual to meet him and engage in memory building. Pick up the phone more often and call your parents and friends to ask about them. Have another child and love the child as much as you can. Take your sister to dinner regularly and speak to her about her and her life. Have an open ear and listen. Cease judging those around you and accept them with love. Every minute you invest in them, they will pay you back. Ill feelings you may have developed in the past must find a grave inside you somewhere. Overcome your vanity and ego. Defeat the devil and pursue your loved ones. Give more even if you meet a cold shoulder. Remember that God and the world will reward you tenfold. I kneel and beg you to consider this lesson. Your parents are absolute jewels, no matter what they have done. You must overcome what you harp inside. The beasts of hate, arrogance, greed, judgment, vengeance, and anger will only destroy you at the end. Believe me; ask the many millionaires I met who are completely alone, without a sound, keeping the AM radio on 24/7 to make sure that they are alive.

We often become deep in debt and slaves to the monthly commitments that we have created with our own selfish greed in the first place. Our intense desire for more is what leads to our eventual slavery. When you are hijacked by the material world and the slavery of monthly commitments, you fall deeper into your internal coma. Your inner awakening to life's true meanings and beauty will come to a complete shutdown. That's why the only pleasures you will ever derive or experience will always be short lived and never, ever fulfilling.

* * *

Messenger of Islam Mohammad Peace Be upon Him once said to one of his companions, "I swear by that who holds my soul in his hand (referring to God), for a man to take a rope, break logs of wood, and then carry it on his back, giving it away for free to people, is far greater than asking for a loan." The power to control the beast of earthly desires further awakens the power within.

These secrets are designed to help you overcome the materialistic traits inside you to lift you to a higher you. The current disaster in the global economy is the result of over-borrowing at every level, and the borrowing was always done for selfish deeds.

* * *

Chapter 2: Asceticism

Asceticism is the decision to desire less by gaining control over your senses. This is the path of greater men and women that walked the face of earth. The one secret you will come to appreciate is that when you become the master of your senses and train yourself to desire less from the world, the world will flock to you.

Asceticism does not mean that you must live a life of scarcity. On the contrary, the very fact that you are capable of controlling the desire of your physical senses means that the smallest fortunes become great before your eyes. This high level of appreciation will further attract more wealth and power your way.

On your way to better, bigger, and more valuable possessions, asceticism will certainly help you remain content and happy, so that you truly enjoy the moments of life you lead even while there is scarcity on the material side. Contentment and joy in the moment coupled with the eventual achievement of the goals you desire results in total success.

The majority of us are born with either mediocre or scarce means with which to work. In fact, many who are born into wealthy families throughout history have suffered trying to create their identity beyond the shadow of their parents. No man is fooled into thinking that the success of his father is his own, at least in the eyes of others. We all seek objectives and goals in the far distance, and living life in misery while seeking higher goals is the greatest source of pain for millions of people around the world. It is also not a secret that many die without achievement. No one can deny that fact. Furthermore, there are institutions out there in the world designed to crush the masses and provide for the elite. While we all must seek a higher financial position for a better materialistic life, we cannot bet everything on some future point in time to be happy.

My mother used to say, "Enjoy your cup of coffee in the morning, appreciate it, and live the moment, for it will never come back." To be happy now, this moment, despite any shortcomings in your life is absolutely possible and doable. It is done through an instant decision to stop grinding your teeth, squeezing your fists, and shaking your legs now, at this particular moment. Try it now. Take an inner decision and command your inner self to relax, your body to go from tense to loose, and look at your inner conflicting thoughts with a sense of separation. Become detached from strings of thinking, and allow the power within to command your deepest stillness.

* * *

I cannot deny that fear can take absolute hold of any of us. As humans, we are aware of the risks that surround us. We have financial obligations and often fall in the trap of greed and arrogance, increasing the pressures on ourselves. Life today offers a multitude of services and products to consume. Everyone around us is indulging one way or another, and we are only human to want to experience these pleasures. We often live beyond our means, and the system does not allow breathing room when personal disaster happens. Nevertheless, fear can claim any of us at any time. My suggestion is to accept it for a moment and move on. You cannot continue to live in the future. If the mortgage payment is due in ten days and you lack the money, what will your frustration, anger, anxiety, or fear serve? If anything, these feelings will only rob you of the energy you need to solve the problem.

Constantly focusing on threats and possible disasters can make any life unbearable. You possess the intellect and the ability to turn inwards and calm yourself down. Again, Begin by taking a very deep breath, and ask your internal body to send signals of assurance and calm. This is not some crazy voodoo exercise; it is a reasonable exercise that promotes calm within you.

Imagine that you are certain a disaster will happen in a few weeks. If you continue to live each moment in pain knowing that this disaster will take place, what will truly happen? Two things:

1. You will have lived in misery, stress, and frustration up to that moment of time, losing days of your life.
2. The disaster, no matter how deep, might never happen, and if did it will pass.

While visiting a prospect from one of my many public seminars, he shared with me the story of the death of his thirty-six-year-old son. His son was married and his marriage was constantly on the rocks, with endless arguments and an eventual decision by the wife to leave. His son took his own life by hanging himself. As I looked in shock and sympathy to the father, witnessing how his eyes reacted as he told the story, I asked, "Why?" In fact we all ask why? Why do people take their own life? What on earth could push someone to commit such a horrific act?

The father said, "I am not sure, but I think he couldn't imagine his life separated from his wife." If that was the true reason, his son was overtaken by fear of the pain of separation. He must have imagined the following scenarios:

- I can't imagine what people would say.
- I will never find another lady who would love me.
- I am a loser.
- I will lose money, time, and my place to live.
- I cannot tolerate the thought that she will eventually be with another man.
- Who would want to be with a thirty-six-year-old man?

These thoughts are fear based. The fear of becoming incapable of tolerating all the changes to come because of the eventual separation took complete hold of his mind and hijacked every moment of his life. These fears lead him to escape through the most horrific of exits.

No one at age nine says to himself, "I will commit suicide one day." But behold, it happens. We all die someday. Why do some end it sooner? It is because we are not trained to be happy, because we fear we will not be able to satisfy the desires of our senses, which are multiplied by our greed and arrogance. In fact, as you reach a level of total fear and inner pain, the body terminates itself as it knows no other means by which it can cure itself. You have trained your inner world to fall for the pressures of the external world. Asceticism is the cure for these illnesses, and the sooner you begin to implement the strategies of asceticism, the sooner you will begin to enjoy life through good times and bad. Remember, your life today is the sum of all the decisions you took, based on your desires and intentions. To reshape your life, you must reshape your decisions and desires.

***

On the path to the higher self, you must observe certain duties. Even any honourable action on your part done excessively will eventually cost you a great deal. I will explain shortly what I mean. In the case of evil actions, one must refrain completely to the best of one's ability, and any evil actions that manifest due to an inner autopilot state should always be brought under control. This discipline of restraint shall help you overcome the evil that lurks inside.

I am a strict believer in changing our patterns over time, and increasing our good deeds slowly but steadily. Consistency in exercising small acts of kindness and goodness will last forever and grow, while great acts of kindness cannot be sustained, and you might stop all the good you do due to it becoming a heavy burden.

The desires of the senses are impossible to fulfill, and it is an everlasting voyage of indulgence throughout our time on earth. The solution for a stronger inner self comes from the art of disentanglement from the material world. This is achieved by following a set of rules that you will create to curb the constant consumption the senses are constantly immersed in.

To achieve a stage of inner strength and self-mastery, one must master all five domains of the senses. This includes the following practices:

- Silence
- Solitude
- Fasting
- Darkness
- Physical contact

The rules

You are not a monk, nor do you want the status of a monk, therefore these activities are to be done for short, specific periods of time to produce the most desirable results.

You must not boast to others about these actions on your part, nor should you do them to impress anyone in your circle. Personal awakening is a private matter and can be transferred to others in due time.

If you find with time that you are highly attracted to one or more domain, you must not allow it to hijack you. Remember, the whole objective of this book is bringing you into balance, control, and inner awakening, not to place you into an extreme opposite state.

- I would befriend a farmer before I would befriend a monk and not the other way around.
- Learn to do before you learn not to do.
- After emerging from any of the following exercises, write down any epiphanies you might have encountered.

- You must not start these exercises when you are in a very engaged state, such as being in a board meeting or while preparing corporate taxes.
- You cannot exercise these methods when others are addressing you or when you are among a social circle where your participation is required. This is respect for those around you who are still dwelling in the hijacked mind.
- The ability to do these exercises while in the presence of others is a different type of mastery, which you will come to understand as you master the initial stages towards sage-hood.

The five senses are gates of purpose. These gates open to your internal world in various ways.

1. Energy: food, nutrition, water, positive reinforcement
2. Protection: danger, threats, information, tools, communication
3. Pleasure: taste, sex, relaxation, higher wisdom, poetry, music, mental power
4. Information: knowledge, wisdom, needs, rules, intelligence, secrets, external thoughts
5. Confirmation: experimentation, positive reinforcement, place, direction, confidence
6. Positioning: advancement, involvement, constructing, advancing, evolving, accumulating

The above is a simple list of duties and derivatives of the senses. Feel free to expand on or reflect upon them as you wish. The goal of the outlines is to explain two things:

1. The complexity of the pressures you face as a human
2. The causes behind many of your thoughts

When we come to understand and observe our constant daily pressures, demands, duties, needs, involvement, communications, feelings, reactions, and exertions, we begin to understand part of the reason for our inner turmoil, anxiety, depression, irritability, low energy, illness, hesitation, fear, insecurity, and pain, and we realize why we seek harmful aids to overcome these horrible inner beasts. The illnesses mentioned above are no more than your inner world sending you signals warning you to change your thought process, as well as your reaction models to external pressures.

Can you see fear or anxiety? Can you taste depression? Can you put your hands around the shoulders of your stress? The answer is of course not. Yet these invisible inner forces are dictating the quality of your life and causing you pain and suffering. To overcome these forces within you, you must do the following:

- Reduce the exposure of your five senses to all things external.
- Refocus your attention inwards.
- Realign your mind with your heart, meaning that what you do must be acceptable by your mind and

your heart. The mind is the domain of logic, and the heart is the domain of morality.
- Examine and reflect on your life as a whole.

The following are suggestions that you may implement regularly (but not constantly) and in small quantities to bring yourself to a state of healing, allowing your higher self to take shape. You cannot build upon a shaky foundation. A false higher self with no inner foundation will certainly crumble faster than one-hundred-year-old structure.

This is exactly why chemicals should be used only in extreme cases. Also, if you do chemically induce a state of peace, you should use this opportunity to address the external deficiencies in your life. Otherwise, medical chemicals will become a permanent aid in facing life's pressures, and this addiction will lead to your physical deterioration.

In order to become whole again, it is important to exercise regular control over the five domains I mentioned above. Here is a sample suggestion to follow. Remember, you should be involved in creating your own program that suits your life and circumstances.

TUESDAY	Sit for 60 minutes alone in a dark room and repeat the phrase "Everything is okay" while breathing deeply with your eyes closed.
THURSDAY	Avoid saying the word "I" for two hours while with others. If you slip, start the timer again. All words are acceptable except the word "I." This exercise shifts our focus towards others, enabling us to focus on what others want, feel, and seek. Mastering this art will make you a centre of attraction and allow you the freedom not to always think about yourself.
SATURDAY	Sit down alone in your room for 20 minutes, observing complete silence. No talking, no radio, no TV—simply focus on your breathing.
SUNDAY	When you wake up, brush your teeth and abstain from eating or drinking anything for 2 hours; increase to 3, 4, 5, 6, 7, and up to 8 hours as you become stronger with time. It is crucial that you do not even drink water. Nothing goes in at all. Once you break the fast, start with a big glass of water.
ONCE A MONTH	Spend a whole day from dawn till night alone. Choose a place that is calm, preferably with a beautiful view. You can eat, listen to soft music, read a book, and walk if you wish. Turn off your cell phone.

ONCE A MONTH	Try not to touch anything or anybody. No sex, no games, no remote control, no books, nothing except food.
ONCE A MONTH	Buy a book and give the book away to a stranger in the street as a gift.

These exercises will help prepare you for inner awakening and serve as the first solid steps towards a higher state of existence—a *higher you.*

Chapter 3: Water-Based Living

"Life's trials are nothing more than a mirage believed to be real by those who failed." —LR

The universe is composed of elements. Each element has its unique characters and attributes. When they combine, they take on new properties and characteristics, representing to us the power of cooperation.

Water is composed of both hydrogen and oxygen. Its symbol on the chart is H2O. Water is the **source** of life. Our body is composed of a large quantity of water—almost 60 percent in the male body and roughly 56 percent in the female body. Water allows the muscle tissue to function, gives bones their unique composition, and comprises most of the blood that runs in our veins (95 percent).

Water is an integral part of life. When you **observe** an element of such importance, you are struck by the simple attributes and character water carries. Water is easily penetrated and manipulated, and it reacts easily to heat and cold. Water also is easily influenced by environmental influences and when mixed with other elements, and it can be recycled back to purity through a simple process.

While I am not aiming to give you a lesson in chemistry (or explain the obvious to you), I am interested in enticing you to begin the habit of observing and reflecting. In an ego-driven world based on the accumulation of material things, one must indulge regularly in the art of reflective attention.

The characters and attributes of water offer tremendously valuable lessons that you can incorporate into your daily life. Water, with its soft texture and tame nature, can over time carve stones, ruin villages, flip ships, kill, or turn a forest into a desert when it is no longer available.

How can you incorporate the character of water and its traits into your own life? And what is so useful about observing the characters of the elements around us? The answer is obvious, but it varies from one individual to another. Water teaches us the *soft approach* and *patience*. As soft as it is, over time, water is able to carve through rocks; in fact, it possesses the power to carve through any solid material over time. The lesson for us is not to give up and to constantly apply the soft approach, starting with ourselves. We should refrain from being so demanding of ourselves and in turn stop being so demanding from life. Demands lead to resistance. Perhaps you have experienced this if you have tried to force a child to do something. The school of positive thought suggests that *leading* a child is far more effective. Likewise, allowing people to love us is not the same as forcing them to love us. The concept applies to almost every aspect of our daily living.

While water is soft, it does not give up on the task it seeks. When water comes in contact with other elements, it may become tainted and discoloured, but it can always return to its original pure state, as it evaporates and returns to the sky from whence it came. You must learn to know how to create your own purification process and how to return through that process to your pure state.

When you were born, you had no anxiety, depression, frustrations, withdrawals, anger, envy, greed, dark intentions, or need for revenge. You must understand that, as with water, your daily interactions with the world as you pass through time does cause you to discolour, and you are bound to become tainted by your daily friction with people, job duties, spouse, money, TV, radio, politics, community, and global events. Your mind, this incredible vessel, has been arranged in a manner that retains a large sum of information in the form of memories. Whether you call it experience, learning, skills, experiments, or maturity, this information will change you each day you walk on this earth.

These changes, regardless of whether they are positive or negative, alter your initial material state at birth. While it is almost impossible to return to such a state—this requires sage-hood, the pinnacle of wisdom hood—you can learn to let go and to purify your body and mind from these daily influences. How, you ask? *The answer is simply by choosing to do so. You are the creator of your inner thoughts, and you are the creator of your inner responses, which are created to aid you in reacting to the external world.*

* * *

Your inner thoughts can be a gift or can be your damnation and misery on earth. The greatest pill of purity is the two simple words: "so what." If you learn to say "so what" combining the words with true inner feelings of care-less-ness, you have arrived to the shore of greatness, my dear friend. This is the element of control. This is the secret behind every secret. Contrary to popular belief that teaches you to control your inner world by ignoring your thoughts and feelings, I am suggesting that you discolour and influence your negative inner thoughts by mixing them with the antibody called, "so what."

A man in prison does not suffer because he is unable to have his freedom—to go shopping, to indulge in the pleasures of the world—but he suffers because he *wants to* have his freedom. Wanting is what causes pain; therefore, we must learn not to want at all. Perhaps you are thinking, "That's insane. How could anyone not want anything?" My reply naturally is that only when you learn to cease to want will the world come to you with all its richness.

Just like you, I have desires, needs, aspirations, ambitions, goals, and a life I always envisioned. The only difference is that I learned that the ultimate secret of achieving all that I want to achieve is *not* desiring, wanting, wishing, aspiring, goal setting, and envisioning, but simply *acting*.

Action is the mechanism of change, change attracts opportunities, and opportunities are the gateway to riches. When you achieve all you have ever wanted to achieve without even wanting it badly, the end result will be a life without inner pain. Your daily existence has become a vessel that accumulates all the germs and infections of the world. You have allowed this to happen, and only you can learn how to purify yourself.

When man is scattered inside, he is in pain, and when he goes through any experience in life, he is affected, regardless of whether the experience is negative or positive. Every conversation you ever had, every show you ever watched, every partner you ever engaged with, every job you ever worked at, every party you ever attended, every drink you ever consumed, every conflict you ever faced, every loss you ever experienced, and every goal you ever accomplished took something from you and gave back something else foreign to your inner world.

Your inner mind has now become a body filled with toxic thoughts, and an endless inner conversation ensues minute by minute, day by day, week by week, month by month, year by year, until you either run yourself into an early grave or open the floodgate and let it all out. Say, "So what?" and open that door now.

Chapter 4: Build Inner Wealth

It seems everyone is intensely interested in wealth these days. One look at the headlines confirms this. I have been immersed in this world for some time now. At the investment company where I worked, daily production numbers were published to fuel the competitive edge between advisors. Closing the sale became the only thing that mattered, and even if you were earning a substantial level of income, it was never enough. Part of the demise of the financial services industry is long overdue, because it is insanely obsessed with profits. I was always shocked to see advisors recruited who never even finished a university degree—only requirement was a high school diploma and a regulator's exam.

This competition created an environment in which jealousy, malice, betrayal, and greed festered. When I left, advisors that I had recruited, trained, and at times protected from being fired were afraid to come and say good-bye to me while I was packing, fearing upper management. I am talking about grown-up men and women. These were advisors who used to dine in my home, share their most intimate problems with me, and seek my help. Many were indebted to me for their success. All of that was a facade. Nothing was genuine, a reflection of what humans can become when they are nurtured in an environment of greed.

I do not mention these elements to express inner anger or disappointment. This all took place back in the nineties, and besides, I am indebted to these circumstances for my awakening. What matters are the lessons derived from this lower, self-promoting environment. It is a reminder to pay attention to your environment, as it can affect you easily while you are in a state of heedlessness. In our insane frenzy for material gain, how often do we step back and take a full account of our *inner wealth?*

As we have allowed our absolute materialistic slavery to fester, we have become unaware of the extent of our inner damage. We have become caught in a vicious cycle that fuels our complete indifference to the source of our ultimate happiness.

It is essential to stop for a moment and begin a serious conversation with your inner self. It is important that you never ever let go of your position as the master of your inner domain and the captain of your thoughts. It is only when you realize that every thought and every impulse inside you does not represent who you truly are that you will you awaken to self mastery. The beginning of awakening is the declaration that *you* are in control and *you* will dictate how you will react to any external event or factor.

Appoint yourself as the judge of your own inner supreme court. It is not an option but a necessity. I guarantee you this: even if circumstances, even if the whole universe collaborates in your financial success, unless you become a true master of your inner self, you will come face to face with your destruction—be it financial, mental, or physical.

"Broke men are not necessarily broken men; wealthy men can be the most broken people you would ever meet." —LR

Do not be fooled by the facade around you. The smiles you see and laugh's you hear are mostly masks that hide inner pains, insecurities, and voids in dire need for fulfillment.

You must accept that mastery is a lifetime project, not a goal to achieve in one month, and that is the beauty of the whole journey towards mastery. The step-by-step awakening to personal power is a joy by itself. Sudden shocks to the system do not work, but slow corrective thinking pattern will have amazing results.

All instant and fast solutions place an enormous pressure on the body and further induce a state of mental confusion and stress. When we constantly seek immediate and fast solutions to problems accumulated over a lifetime, we *further teach our bodies and souls to expect faster solutions.* This becomes an illness by itself, producing stress, low self-esteem, unhappiness, frustration, and confusion when we fail to realize immediate change. We are on earth for a limited time only. Even a man behind bars realizes that one day he will be free, whether at the end of his prison term or the end of his life. No one can hold you prisoner except you. You are the only true prisoner of your free self. No one can make you sad, upset, frustrated, or angry unless you allow them to do so. When you master this idea, you become a powerful human being.

When you are awakened, you realize that you are so blessed with inner riches, the world for you is nothing more than a solid mirage. We must look for internal wealth and rely on no exterior confirmations. This is all possible if we take the time to observe our inner conversations and the battle between our inner desires and feelings. With every passing day, your higher self becomes stronger and the battle inside you will slowly subside.

Chapter 5: The Path to Sage-hood

We do most of what we do in the hope of achieving some distant happiness. We believe that the accumulation of wealth for example will make us happy in some distant moment in the future. The truth is this: happiness and contentment can be felt this very second. Happiness is the ability to have clarity of mind and complete serenity despite the storm of life. This is what we call sage-hood.

Sage-hood is not a constant, for even prophets felt sad and were shaken at times or frustrated with those who rejected their message. Sages would cry when they lost a loved one at the same time that they preached that everything was an illusion. I would like for you to aim towards achieving moments of sage-hood. These moments will grow with time. Learn how to command your mind to stop thinking. Learn to smile and feel joy whenever you decide to summon such a feeling. Realize that any mental, external trap you're facing can never last forever, and it cannot overcome you unless you accept defeat. You have the ability to see the weakness of life as it is, and you are free despite all the shackles.

We are the creators of our jails on earth—they are our uncontrollable desires. We allow our world to close in on us. While it happens to the best of us, we also possess the power to cease to engage. You have the ability within you to observe your thoughts and respond to them (as, after all, they are just thoughts). You have decided not to allow these thoughts to trigger your inner frustration.

Life will never cease to offer you challenges and problems. This is the nature of life, and this is particularly the case since we are surrounded by other egos. You are responsible for controlling how you feel about everything around you. The previous chapters aided you in the path of inner cleansing to help you reach this moment of sage-hood and the ability to smile in the face of the worst moments.

In an instant, you can decide not to be angry, frustrated, unhappy, afraid, or lost. Try it at least once, perhaps when you come face to face with your next challenge. Say it and *feel* that you will not be engaged in your negative feelings. This ability is priceless, but like all good things, it comes through effort, and in stages.

The first step on the path to sage-hood is the mastery of stillness. Following this is the dreamer state, the fountain from which goals—when coupled with action and the blessing of the divine—begin to appear in your physical life. Once you master this state, I will help take you to the noble stage. The noble stage is when you bring you attention to everything that is noble, good, and positive. It is a meditative stage where you allow pure thoughts to enter and deny access to negative or intrusive stress. Once you have progressed through these states, you will have reached the stage of sage-hood, a realm of deep internal calm.

* * *

Stillness

In this first stage on the path to sage-hood, you will develop the ability to sit still, without movement, words, food, or noise, starting in increments of a few minutes and gradually working to up to five hours of complete wakeful stillness. You can shift your body to avoid numbness, and sitting on a big cushion or on your bed might help. The exercise requires a technique called "brushing the mind," in which you allow your thoughts pass by without resistance and delete them without resistance or stress. Breathing is a major component of the exercise, as you can focus on this one bodily function whenever your mind wanders. The ultimate objective is to reach a state of complete stillness, calmness, and physical comfort. Once you have achieved this task, congratulations, you have begun your mastery of internal control.

* * *

Dreamer state

This is an important exercise, because you must be looking for material success in your life. As I said before, this book was never meant to neglect the physical experience of your life; you are healthy in perusing physical goals such as a loving relationship, a beautiful home, a fulfilling career, and a secure retirement. To be able to travel, experience, interact, give, build, and grow, you require a certain level of material success. You must select the level of riches you want to achieve, and you must remember to do this in a noble domain and in the service of others. Do not do it to prove yourself to the world or to seek anyone's acceptance. I know many people who choose a much simpler life, with limited resources and focused on living rather than spending the limited hours of their life building material wealth. Choose what suites you and what will ultimately make you free. Wealth can be as enslaving as poverty—that is why extremism is always rejected.

In this meditative stage, you will sit relaxed and focus inwards. You will search for the proper mental picture that describes your objective. Let me give you an example:

I see myself arriving at my home. It is a beautiful home, painted white with a large driveway and scattered with trees on each side. I see my wife talking on the phone and my children playing in the backyard. I see the marble tiles on the floor clearly and the big modern kitchen. The dining table, with twelve chairs, is made out of solid oak, and I have a big English clock standing on the left side in the guest room. The carpet in the guest room light in color, and I can touch the carpet with my own hands. I kiss my wife and go up the stairs to my room to change. I see my king-size bed, surrounded with light white drapes falling from the ceiling. I undress and slip into the shower. Every time I go to my washroom, I am amazed at the size. It is bigger than the whole apartment I used to rent downtown. Done with the shower, I see myself performing my prayers and then going down to join my family for dinner. My wife goes on and on about her day at work, and I keep poking at my son. She doesn't like that, and she gives us a lesson on table manners. We then finish and help clean off the table, and then we rush outside to play some basketball. I have a great time with my kids. We then wash up and help the kids with homework. The wife and I watch TV, and then I read and fall asleep.

You will create your own vision. It could be career related, a painting in your mind with details of how your day looks. You can visualize your bank account and the number you would like to see in it. You could see yourself working hard at the details towards your specific goal.

Remember to follow the following tips to ensure a higher rate of success:

- Include as many details as possible.
- Ensure that you touch with your inner hand the walls, the carpet, the desk, and the papers on the desk; feel the handshakes and focus on the colors of everything around you.
- Once you are satisfied with the picture, take five minutes daily to sit still and see that picture again and again.
- Visualise the steps needed to achieve your goals.
- See yourself doing all that is needed through your mind.
- See yourself making an internal decision to achieve these goals.
- Write these decisions on a piece of paper.
- Begin real, material action.
- Ask God for help, and pray for his blessings.

* * *

Noble stage

This meditation level is what I call the filtering stage. Spend as little as five minutes in complete stillness and focus on all that is good. See yourself giving to the poor, helping an old man cross the street, helping a single mother find a job, listening to your friends' problems, eating healthier food, stopping alcoholic consumption completely, reducing your intake of medical drugs, writing an essay on love, attending family gatherings, forgiving those that trespassed against you, healing old wounds, forgiving old foes, praying with complete respect, turning your back on deceit, motivating others to overcome obstacles, giving respect to every living being—even the mosquito, seeing those you feel jealousy towards achieve more than you and feeling happy for them, helping someone achieve a dream, forgiving your spouse for his or her shortcomings, reconnecting with family members, sending internal messages of love and peace, shedding your selfishness, eliminating your arrogance, increasing your humbleness, visualizing your smile, clearing your heart of the world, uniting with your peaceful inner self, gently pushing all your fears aside, touching your anxiety with your fingertips and seeing it crumble, squeezing your depression with your fist slowly and seeing it dissolve, seeing your trust grow in the future, seeing your world at peace, seeing your uniqueness, opening the tap of your inner confidence, filling your heart with joy, feeling your energy field grow, seeing yourself a magnate to greatness, observing the eye of the universe focused on you coming closer, feeling the surrender to the power of God, and believing in the ability to shine again, soon, for certain.

"In a moment of silence, I can see the whole earth in my palm—so small, so fragile—and then, immediately, I see my insignificance. I am smaller than a black ant in the sight of God." —LR

***

The stage of sage-hood

This stage is a moment and an eternity. Sage-hood is the ability to separate feelings from thoughts, the ability not to be affected by the external and to dwell in internal calm. This is the stage of revealing the fragility of life and the pleasure of the present moment. It is the detachment from desire and the attachment to inner pleasure. It is the calm *within* the storm. Think of the story of Moses parting the Red Sea. You have this ability within yourself—it is the ability to say to your mind, "Stop," and seeing it stop. You are becoming a commander, saying to your inner world, "No, I will not feel this pain," and it miraculously happens. I do it myself; it works, and it's amazing. I can be in a state of deep stress, and then remember and command myself not to be stressed and my face instantly relaxes and calm descends upon me. This form of surrender and ease is present within each and every one of us. We simply need to take back control from the external afflicter and become the deciders of our moods and feelings. It doesn't happen easily until one understands that one's inner thoughts are not necessarily one's inner feelings. The thoughts will remain, but how you respond is determined by the deep inner you, the experiencing soul. Why engage? Disengage, decide, command it, and it shall be.

"There comes a moment for the awakened, when they live under every stone, every particle of dust, in every water stream, in every river and ocean, in every tear, smile, and devoted hand, in the roots of a tree, and in the heart of others." —LR

Conclusion

This section was an attempt to help you redirect your attention inwards, show you the inner conflict, explain the origin of your slavery, and point you toward a very powerful question: "Are you worthy of greatness?" You must begin by controlling your inner world, and you must reclaim your hijacked self and repossess your post as the judge on your supreme court. To do that, you must open your inner eyes and bring your focus to your inner dialogue and manifesting feelings. I will touch on this fundamental point throughout this book, and your understanding of this concept will grow as you read these pages. To become great, you must be worthy of becoming great, and in becoming worthy of greatness you must open your eyes to the inner forces of constructive good in you.

You will fail many times on the path of reclaiming yourself, but every time you bring your attention to this internal dialogue, you will become stronger. With time, you will regain mastery of yourself and begin to dictate your responses and your behaviour. Yes, it is as simple as that. Once you begin, you are now among the 10 percent of people in this world who are in this category. You have decided to jump out of heedlessness to a state of awakening to the inner truth, and you have embarked on a journey of self-discovery and control. You have begun to observe how desires and feelings are battling inside you. The very fact that you have begun such a process is the beginning of an amazing journey within.

PART 2: LESSONS FROM THE PAST

The men and women who walked Mother Earth so long ago were not as busy as we are today. They had time for reflection and self-assessment. Their mind was not occupied with many of the distractions and stresses of today's world. We live in a world that is fast and furious. We rarely have time for our bodies to rest, never mind our minds to reflect. The wisdom derived from the reflection of the men before us is rich and valuable. I read some bestsellers today and find that the content has already been summarized in a single chapter of a nine-hundred-year-old book or a conversation between two wise men documented fourteen hundred years ago.

The past was also the era of prophets, many of whom brought a message of hope, change, and advancement. Most of our beliefs concerning life after death, as well as much of today's morality originated thousands of years ago. Man's search for reason and hope started in the Far East, travelling to the Middle East and eventually to the western side of the world.

We are relatively young in the progression of our subconscious mind, lacking the deep inner wisdom that men of the past possessed. Today, we are obsessed with science and advancement. We seek inventions of comfort and develop inventions of destructions. C. G. Jung, the German psychologist, put this notion beautifully, saying that man today is no less evil or destructive than man of the old ages. The only difference is that man today has developed weapons that could literally obliterate half the earth.

The truth is we are all equally responsible as individuals to seek the improvement of our inner world. To pursue knowledge of the self is an honourable, commendable exercise needed for lifting up society as a whole. The global village we live in is in dire need of fresh concepts based on old wisdom to advance peace, both internal and external.

Our children also need to go back in time and study what men of the past said. The great sages of the past each carried a unique message of love, equality, and worldly detachment for a sane existance. Our intensely materialistic existence contaminates our souls and minds with the poison of pain, hate, and stress. When we reach inner peace, we can manifest greater philosophies and better laws to propel our world forward based on Godly laws sent through prophetic revelations. Obsession with the rights and privileges of the one, the state, the nation, and the race are the cause of much of the pain we continue to endure.

We all have dreams, aspirations, and feelings. We all need belonging, and to build a better life in a peaceful land. But we can only progress when we take a moment in time to reflect and invest in our deep self. The following stories stand as a witness to the strength of the human spirit, the weakness of the ego, the power of the righteous deed, and the wisdom of change from within. I hope that when you read these stories, you will find yourself reflecting on the meaning within and begin to incorporate some of the concepts into your inner world.

Chapter 6: The Apple

Hundreds of years ago, a young man was passing beside a big fenced land. Apple trees stood close to the fence. The man saw an apple that fell from one of the trees growing near the edge of the fence. He picked up the apple, cleaned it, and took a big bite. While he was chewing, he suddenly realized that he had committed an offence. A voice inside his head told him that he just took what wasn't his. The young man felt guilty and rushed to the gate of the fenced land. At the gate sat a man gazing at the open fields. The young man who ate part of the apple greeted the man at the gate and admitted the guilt he felt for eating part of the apple and asked for forgiveness.

The other man replied, "I cannot grant you what is not mine to grant. I am but a guard in this castle. You must ask forgiveness from the owner." The young man then requested a face-to-face meeting with the owner." The guard rushed in and expressed the wish of the man at the door.

The owner summoned him in and gave the young man a chance to speak. The young man expressed his guilt and apologized for eating the apple, and said that he couldn't face his God after death having committed such a crime. The owner looked on with amazement and said, "But it's only a small apple. Do you really think that God would punish you for it?"

"Certainly," replied the young man. He added, "Whether I took an apple or took your whole land, the act in itself is the same. We are punished based on principles, not the size of the offence."

The owner of the castle was impressed by the honesty, integrity, and intelligence of the young man. After thinking for a while as the young man awaited nervously for forgiveness, the owner of the castle came up with a proposition. He told him that he would forgive him under one condition. The young man nodded. The condition was that the young man must marry the master's daughter. The young man hesitated for a second. Could he really marry a woman he had never seen before in his life? After a few seconds, the young man said, "If you would forgive my transgression so that God will not punish me, I am willing to accept your offer."

The master of the castle said, "You must know that my daughter has a condition. She is blind, deaf, mute, and lame."

The young man began to realize the difficulty of the test, but he thought, *Perhaps she is my path to great rewards from God. As I serve her, I would be serving him.* Then, the young man looked up and said to the master, "I accept your proposal."

The master of the castle ordered the marriage ceremony to commence past midday, and so it went. When the ceremony was finished and the guests went home, the father of the bride took the hand of his new son-in-law, walked him to a smaller house on the eastern side of the castle, and told him to go to his bride, where she awaited him and where he and she would live.

The young man walked to the door and entered. As he entered, he placed his cape on the side of the door and uttered words of greeting. A soft voice replied with a warmer greeting. He was shocked and looked perplexed. The bride said, "What has come unto you? Do you not like me?"

The young man said, "On the contrary, but I never thought your father would be the kind of man to lie."

She replied, "You are correct. My father is a righteous man who would never do such a thing, and lying he never did."

The young man said, "But he told me that you were blind, deaf, mute, and lame, but when I look at you, I see beauty, I hear your sweet voice, and I see you stand on your own two feet."

The young bride answered with a smile, "My father was right, you see. I am blind before the sight of evil, deaf when the words of evil are uttered, unable to speak evil, and unable to walk towards evil."

The young man smiled and knew at this moment that he was a very lucky man. His bride had beauty, grace, wisdom, knowledge, and love. They later on had a child, who became a wise man, renewing the sciences of religion and faith. The son's name was Abu Hanifah Alnu'mnan, a historical scholar in Arabia.

This is a true story

When I first came face to face with this story, I couldn't help but notice the deep wisdom within it. It sparked the beauty and rewards that come with doing the right thing. Would you have done what this young man did to correct a wrong? I certainly would have found it a very difficult test, unless I had a sense of deep wisdom and deep morality. This is a testimony to what is hidden behind every moral stop sign we come to pass.

How often have we committed such "slight" transgressions as taking a newspaper from a cafe when we leave or not returning an extra quarter mistakenly given to us by the teller at the shop? How often have we committed bigger sins, such as lying to clients and customers or to our spouses and friends? Once we begin to lie to ourselves, to justify what we do, we fall deep into a hellish existence that we refuse to face up to. We live in an age where if anyone speaks about integrity, about truth, about honesty, he is shouted down as sanctimonious or as a hypocrite. It is easy to poke holes in those who are righteous by making the excuse that certain actions are necessary to survive in a cruel world.

Sometimes, on the surface, I find myself agreeing. You look and find that riches and power are often in the hands of the corrupt and the twisted. We endure the fallacy of it all, because we think that this is the path. We are in a race against time and in constant motion to rewind the tape of the years, and we are simply expressing our dear disappointment in the material world. When what is inside is completely destroyed, we hang on the drapes of the exterior world. The face of a seventy-year-old woman reconstructed twenty times through plastic surgery is an example of such desperate clinging. Yet, our grip weakens with time, and we all fall. Only the young inside and only the healed inside shall swim with the angels when the material ride is over.

* * *

Chapter 7: Seek Beauty

When a few of Jesus' friends (peace be upon him) walked with him one day, they came across a dead animal that had been there for quite some time. The site was so ugly, filthy, and disgusting that everyone began to express their repugnance with the site and the animal.

However, Jesus looked on and said, **"Look how bright and clean his teeth are."**

To seek the higher self, you must shed light on the beauty of your deepest inner self. The beauty is always there despite our autopilot's best effort to distract us from it. You have been running on autopilots since you were a child, and the majority of these are destructive habits. When you reflect inwards, you re-engage in the decision-making process. Look at the dialogue inside you between your desire and your reason. You must allow reason and good to overcome the ill excess of desire. No one is asking you to change instantly, but to at least begin the journey of inner correction. This is done by siding with the voice of reason and balance, which lies inside you but is weakened by years of neglect. That's why we smoke, over-drink, gamble, get angry, overeat, oversleep, waste hours in front the TV, and engage in other useless, harmful behaviours. One of our automatic responses to this world is to identify ugliness; it is difficult to see beauty in everything, but this is one of the choices we must make.

* * *

It was narrated that the prophet Mohammad (peace be upon him) said, **"God does not look at your bodies or external beauty. God looks at your hearts."** That is simply because true beauty is on the inside. I can hide the worst of intentions and the bleakest of dimensions within my inner self only to fool the world with my external appearance and actions. The truth about what you are and who you are is the summation of what lurks inside your heart. While you continue hard to cover up the inside world you command, sooner or later it surfaces and reflects on your exterior existance. They say you would only know a man when you travel with him a long journey, and you would only know a woman when she hates. Seeking the refinement of both the internal and the external aspects of our short existence is, in my humble opinion, a task to which we must all set ourselves.

* * *

Where there is ugliness, create beauty

As I have said, it is not enough to want goodness; we must *act* to create it in our world. Prophet of Islam Muhammad said, "Whoever amongst you sees an ill or a corrupt act, he must change it with his own hands, and if he cannot, then change it with his tongue through spoken words, and If he cannot, then with his heart, and that's the weakest of faith." One must act to correct wickedness when he or she can. Everything is connected. If we don't find cures for diseases in Africa and decide not to provide medicine to the ill, we will one day suffer the spread of death. However, I cannot force others to act; therefore, I must do my best to effect change myself. How?

- I must send money when I can.
- I must write my government representatives.
- Finally, I must host wishes of relief and wishes for their healing in my heart.

It is your duty to attract thoughts of goodness towards your inner self and the world. This is something you can do daily. Try to close your eyes in a quiet place for just a few moments (even less than one minute) and repeat words of encouragement to yourself, such as:

- I am more than this physical body.
- I have greatness inside me.
- I can influence my life toward the good.
- I can overcome the evil that lurks within me.
- I can diminish the sound of confusion
- I am conscious to the desire to be a better human being.

Once the minute repeating this message is up, it is time to give to the world by closing your eyes and focusing on the world with words such as:

- I send peace to every broken parent over the loss of their child.
- I send hope to those in despair and in need of a helping hand.

- I send wishes of hope to the people in Africa.
- I send a message of peace and hope for people in the Middle East.
- I send warm wishes of healing for Eastern Europe.
- I send a prayer for the blinded greed in the west.
- I send a wish of healing for the morality of humanity.

These words, internally uttered, grant you access to a noble cause. The very fact that you thought these thoughts and repeated them regularly whenever you got a chance adds to the army of your internal good. It increases the size of your inner bank account as it fills up with positive messages.

Today, I am lucky to claim that I am fully engaged in regular training of my mind, and I constantly observe my internal dialogue. This regular mindfulness is aimed at regaining my lost pinnacle self at birth, returning to some point in my existence when I was purer, happier, and more fulfilled, calm, content, and in control. When I fail again and fall prey to my negative inner world, I smile admitting my weakness, but I try again until I am back in a centred self. Long gone are the days when I would beat myself for long for failing. Today, each failure and each step back is considered a new exercise needed for me to eventually master the art of inner beauty and calm.

* * *

The crippled inner world of most people is clearly evident in our society today. Many brilliant thinkers have touched on this point one way or another, intentionally or by accident, eloquently or in mundane language. The decision makers in our world—from heads of states and economic leaders to the common man and woman—are largely on automatic pilot, existing in a state of heedlessness. You can see it daily in the corruption, greed, wars, assassinations, murder, theft, abuse, anger, hostility, illness, racism, elitism, corruption, hunger, famine, pain, and stress that characterize our world. It is amazing how the people we consider to be the best among us are mostly heading in the wrong direction. Do we blame them, or do we blame their environment, which is merely a reflection of how most of us feel inside?

It is your task and mine to create beauty by elevating oneself from a lower level of existence to a higher one. No change can dawn until the majority of the population of the world is elevated to an awakened state of existence, seeking peace and prosperity for the entire world. But each of us must begin this journey on his or her own.

My decision begins with the exercise of my duty to awaken myself from its deep slumber and perhaps, through this book, yours. I want to see you succeed, prosper, smile, be happier, be more in control, and enjoy every precious moment that life bring to you. I want you to claim the wisdom needed to understand that the dynamic of life is change. Nothing is still. Not even death stops the flow of change. Death is the gateway to the next and final frontier, where we truly belong. If you are not capable of achieving beauty in your life, you will continue to suffer as the world takes you up and then crush you down.

Beware of false beauty

When you drink alcohol, you might experience superficial sensations of physical joy, but this is false beauty, a chimera at best. As time passes, you begin to seek alcohol to numb your senses and to escape reality, and to live in a dimension of false courage and no pain. As time passes, you autopilot self is incapable of escaping from your inner demons and shortcomings, and you deliver yourself to a more intense form of sleep, and that is the state of drunkenness.

Many of the most popular among us engage in self-destructive behaviour as society constantly searches for ways to bring us down. Eckhart Tolle referred to this point when he wrote the story of the Arabian King who, suffering from emotional disturbances, sought a wise old man for help. The help came in the form of a ring that had an engraving on it with the words, "This too shall pass." The actual words on the ring were "The persistence of the present status is impossible." While change is imminent, *you* must take control, before one day you are completely out of control.

A wise man in Arabia was asked, "What possessions do you constantly seek and acquire?"

The wise man replied, "Those things that when my ship sinks would swim with me." The wise man was referring to knowledge. The ship refers to all your positions and wealth. When all is gone, the only thing that remains is your knowledge and wisdom, with which you can always build again. The knowledge of the self is the pursuit of the higher self. A very wise religious man once gave the following advice: "Fix yourself before you fix the world, for your world is a reflection of you." It is of absolute importance that we work on ourselves, creating beauty in our own inner world, before we can emerge.

* * *

Chapter 8: The Bird

A wise man not too long ago had his own gathering place where men of all ages would assemble seeking knowledge and the honourable company of this wise man. With time, they noticed that the wise man had taken a serious interest in a young boy, no more than thirteen years of age. He would pay attention to him, look at him as he taught, and give him extra care. One day, the men complained with humility to the master that they felt they were more worthy of such praise, attention, and respect. After all, they were much older; among them were men even over sixty years of age.

The wise man smiled and said, "I take your concern seriously." Then he looked at everyone in the room and said, "Tomorrow, I want each of you to bring with him a knife and a bird." Everyone in the room looked with astonishment but nodded with agreement out of respect for his stature.

Next day, they all gathered, and each brought a bird and a knife, including the young boy. The master looked at them and said, "Now I want you all to go seek a place of hiding, where you will slaughter the bird. Then you shall return here with the evidence. Make sure no one can see you when you perform the slaughter."

They all dispersed and went seeking a place of refuge from the eyes around them in order to fulfill the order of the master. In roughly thirty minutes, the students started to come back one by one carrying the dead birds with them, placing the slaughtered birds before the master. Then came the young boy of thirteen, to the surprise of every one gathered, carrying the bird alive. The master looked at the boy with an eye of anger and said with a loud voice, "How you dare disobey my orders?"

The young boy replied with confidence, "Master, on the contrary, I have honoured your request, and the live bird is the proof."

"Explain," shouted the master.

The young boy said, "I have looked for a place where no eye can see me slaughter the bird but failed to find such a place. You see, master," he continued, "even if no one here can see me kill the bird, my own eye is a witness, and God can see all."

The men erupted in shock and awe to the insight of the young boy. The master smiled and looked at everyone. "Do you have your answer now?" he said.

This story is a step on the path towards awakening. When you become the first officer to uphold yourself to the highest standards, you begin to grow. You must recognize that every action you take is witnessed first by your own eye and second by the higher force that can see all your deeds. Never assume that your actions go in vain, and never expect that what you do is without consequence.

The sage, the wise, and the awakened arrive at the knowledge that every action is recorded in the field of energy of our existence—nothing is erased or lost. What we do remains, its effects lingering in our universe. Think of the world as a space where every word you say and every action you take changes the spatial dimension of this world. These changes affect us all, directly or indirectly. When a man has deep frustrations and erupts in a hostile argument with his parents, perhaps after a divorce or the loss of his business, and then buys a gun and goes on a shooting rampage, have you anything to do with that? Is he solely responsible for the action? Have people cheated him at work? Did another man seduce his wife? Did his parents abuse him as a child? Was he often bullied and insulted at school? Did society treat him like dirt? While all of this does not alleviate the blame from him, we are all somehow responsible for his actions.

Perhaps someone has done something or said something that has affected you, even while you were not part of that person's circle. The world is filled with victims of other people's madness and mistakes. This is why we must always be mindful of our actions, never assuming that we can commit evil acts without consequence. Every good deed we commit will be rewarded for in due time, and every ill deed shall come to haunt us in due time. We cannot enter the heaven of a peaceful inner existence until we purify our actions, and we will only purify our actions when we purify our inner world.

***

Chapter 9: Seek Knowledge and Act

"The most beautiful addiction is the addiction to knowledge."
—*LR*

What is knowledge? Some say it is power and others say it's the door to wisdom. Many claim it is mastery of a specific topic or an innate exploration of a particular field. The Merriam-Webster dictionary has roughly four definitions of knowledge. The one that captures my attention the most is "Knowledge applies to facts or ideas acquired by study, investigation, observation, or experience (rich in the knowledge of human nature)." The four elements of knowledge are

- Study
- Investigation
- Observation
- Experience

Reading by itself is the beginning of knowledge. It is the gate to a world unknown to you and observed through the eyes of others who wrote about it before you. One must draw a line, however, between reading for knowledge and reading for entertainment. The higher step is the investigation of the validity, credibility, truthfulness, relativity, and its role in serving you and humanity. This is reading opposing views and opinions. When the investigation level is satisfied, you should observe the effect of the knowledge you have acquired upon others or surroundings. Then there is the ultimate knowledge, and that is the knowledge of experience.

Knowledge is a key factor to unlocking the pathways of wisdom. It will not only help you grow spiritually, internally, and mentally, but it will also help you acquire wealth, status, power, or whatever it is you wish to achieve in the ego-driven, material side of your existence. It is crucial to mention that knowledge without experience is dormant unless it is acquired for the sole purpose of acquiring a job, such as teaching. A priest, a sheikh, or a master cannot preach about self-restrain and the way to conquer sin if he or she does not practice what they preach. Imam Ghazali, a high master in Islam nine hundred years ago, said, "The tax of preaching is practicing what you preach." It is truly crucial for you to put what you learn to the test and to experience it firsthand. I am referring to the knowledge of life, wisdom, and disciplines of value. Anthony Robbins' legacy can be summarized by one powerful message and that is *decision and action*. This message is not a new one—it was delivered before him by ancient masters—but the message seems to have been lost in time. We need to bring this mode of thinking back before we sink into a world of materialistic insanity.

As I have said numerous times, *deciding to do something* isn't enough; it will not happen unless you *do something* about it. The phenomenon of "The Secret" seems to have taken the world by storm, yet, almost everyone has ignored that in order to manifest any reality, *action* is required. Allow me to explain. Many self-help giants say that when you focus on something, a goal, and head towards it, the universe collaborates with you and brings forth helping tools and opportunities to achieve such a goal. When I decided to become a motivational speaker, coach, and corporate trainer, I realized that I had been preparing for this goal for the past fourteen years, but it took *action* to make it a reality. Once I decided to do it, my thoughts then turned to solutions to achieving my goal. That in turn brought forth idea after idea, because I had employed my mind to come up with solutions. The mind is the greatest gift we have; however, the ideas it produces, when not followed with action, remain dormant traces of inner energy.

Do you know how many I times I wrote this book in my mind. Do you know how many sleepless nights I spent typing out these chapters in my head? That preparation had its value, but it only began to manifest when I dragged my lazy existence into my den and decided to start typing in earnest after three years of non-action. Even after this book was completed, I could have easily stored it away in my laptop where it would have never seen the light again. If you are reading this book, it means that an enormous effort was invested before it reached your palms. Every step of the way, thoughts arose of quitting, stopping, and letting this dream go. The exhaustion exerted in writing is monumental. It squeezes and drains your mind and tests it to the limit, and it's a process that never really ends. Yet this is no different from any endeavour worth doing—the negative thoughts one has to overcome to pursue any path are enormous. **Success is truly hard work.**

Many great minds have spoken of ways for us to get motivated and to begin doing what we dream about doing. The one problem with most systems is that motivation tends to evaporate shortly after reading a book or listening to a tape.

The one particular system that works for me is the following sentence: **"Time is running out."** I started realizing one day the concept of time. Time is such a precious commodity. We do not realize that the endless days and nights we spend playing, laughing, going out, dreaming, working, watching TV, reading the paper, and drinking our coffee take up the majority of our daily existence.

Picture with me a car that you own. This car was designed to serve a purpose, and that is transportation. In order for your car to function properly, you need to fill it up with gas once a week, change the oil every three months or so, change the tires every two years or so, and maintain it every now and then. These tasks are simple and manageable for the average driver. Now imagine that a car was not as simple to maintain. Imagine that every morning when you wake up, you need to fill the car with gas, change the oil, and change the tires. The car becomes a nightmare—it needs too much effort to maintain, so you begin to look for other means of transportation.

The car in this case still has its purpose, despite the enormity of services it needs to function. Now imagine as an addition to this problem, the car becomes more than a tool for transportation. That the car becomes symbol of your value in society, and therefore you begin to invest heavily in expensive rims, juiced-up engine accessories, daily servicing and checking of parts, and so on. The vehicle has now shifted from its intended original purpose of simply transporting you to your destinations and has become an ego tool. Further, merely to serve its original purpose, it now requires long hours of service and daily replacement of parts.

This nightmare is similar to a man who has shifted from his original purpose and who has become bottled up in daily activities that do nothing more than hinder his progress and waste his valuable time.

I do not raise the spectre of "time running out" to instil fear in you but to remind you of the scarcity of time in relation to what you wish to achieve. My intention is to bring things into perspective and motivate you to focus on your goal. Man was not designed to play all the time, nor was he designed to work all the time; man was designed to serve a noble purpose that would elevate him, elevate those around him, and add to the collective goodness of the earth. Religion teaches us that humanity's purpose is the worship of its creator. Worship does not mean kneeling down and attending religious gatherings only, but to be in a state of worship throughout all you do. Worship means submission in goodness. Goodness means noble actions. Noble actions mean a higher self. A higher self means honour and success. Honour and success is only valuable when its shared and done not on the expense of others.

To achieve all that, you must reflect on how you function on a daily basis. How many hours do you spend sleeping, eating, watching TV, playing video games, talking on the phone, hanging out with friends, sitting in cafes, and seeking entertainment? What else could you be doing with this time? How else could you be applying the knowledge you have acquired in your life? How should you invest the time for a higher purpose?

Greatness begins in childhood

One of our greatest shortcomings is that we have turned our children generations into pure consumers of good time. The amount of time teenagers spend in play from age thirteen to age twenty is a tremendous waste.

Perhaps you are thinking, "Relax. They are children, and they must play." Yes, they can play, but they should not *live to play*. The ten years from age thirteen until the end of university are filled with a massive amount of play for most youth. Then, comes the love story and the sweetheart, the search for a job, the marriage, the mortgage, the children, and then the midlife crisis.

However, the lessons of history teach us that true greatness begins from a young age. A child can memorize at least twenty books by heart by age twenty, and master two or three skills. In fact, from age thirteen to age twenty-three, if a commitment is made to reading—for example, a book every two weeks—a child would reach age twenty-three having read more than 240 books. Can you imagine! Can you contemplate the result! And this is not done to eventually make millions but done to create scholars and wise men and women to elevate the conscious existence of our society, to improve our discoveries in medicine, science, space, manufacturing, technology, spirituality, and life on earth in general.

As you read this, most likely these years are gone for you, and that is all the more reason for you to make the decision to get up and start achieving your goals. Take risks, penetrate your comfort zone, reduce your TV and Internet time, focus, establish your noble cause, write down your objectives, and take the first step forward. I see young men and women, and even middle-aged men and women, spending countless hours in clubs, bars, and restaurants idling time away. Go to any movie theatre and see the worship of entertainment. We are obsessed with the news of celebrities, singers, and athletes. You were not been brought to earth to devote your time to these people.

Men and women become depressed in their thirties and forties because as time passes, they begin to see the emptiness of it all. The endless wine bottles, parties, and good times have passed, leaving them with nothing. They still have no defined purpose, no major objectives, and no major accomplishments to note after all the years that have passed. Further, their relationships are awkward, strange, and painful. Life has become narrower and narrower with each passing day. Ask my client the pharmacist—he told me if he were to stop selling antidepressants, anxiety pills, psychotic pills, and sedatives, he would go out of business. He confessed that 80 percent of medicines sold are related to mental functioning. This is astonishing.

Many men define their value based on the wealth they have amassed or the agility of their bodies; likewise, many women cling to their beauty as that which defines their value. However, all these things are ephemeral; time will pull them away, and eventually they will have nothing left to define them as human beings. As time passes they become a crumbling entity inside. We cannot continue clinging to and wasting time on matters that will one day disappear or evaporate; we must focus on goals that are worthy of the time we were so blessed with on earth.

What is your dream? Tell me your dream and I will tell you who you are. If your dream is money, fame, beauty, a big car, or a huge house, then that is what you are—nothing more than these things, and as they disappear so will you. Now the inventor of electricity, the author of *War and Peace*, the inventor of the PC or insulin, the scholars of the ages, the philosophers, the grand teachers, the prophets, and the angels of mercy are the ones who have achieved. They are immortalized in our consciousness. Those who spent their life going to clubs, drinking, playing, pushing their kids out early from the sanctuary of the family, and accumulating money shall die barely remembered by a few people. Open the paper to the obituaries. Do you recognize any of them? Do you even feel sorry for the loved ones they left behind? The natural answer is no, because most of them did one thing and one thing only—consume their way to the grave.

I admit this may sound harsh. I am a human being, as you are, and I yearn for play and fun and I do it. Yet I regret the endless hours and years wasted on nothing. I could have done so much more. Look at men like Jesus, Moses, and Mohammed (peace be upon them). They spread a message that billions now follow. In less than twenty-three years, Prophet Mohammad was able to establish one of the fastest growing religions in the world—a Bedouin from the desert who was illiterate. You say, "But these were prophets and messengers who were favoured by God," and I would say, yes, but they still worked day and night, focused on their message and their objective. They fulfilled their message and accomplished their task. They have become immortal in our consciousness and shall live until the end of time. Buddha as well spread messages of deep wisdom. His wisdom was so profound that he was revered as a god by millions around the word, and still is to this day. That was Buddha's only mistake, not clarifying who the real creator is for the masses.

The examples are endless, and the message is simple: You posses the seeds of greatness and you have what it takes, no matter what your condition is. All you need to do is define what you want to accomplish, what noble cause for a higher purpose, and begin to work on it immediately, because time is running out, my friend.

* * *

Through the experience of writing this book, I grew more respectful of writers. Those who bring us knowledge and spend endless nights reading, researching, listening, observing, debating, correcting, adjusting, and revisiting are truly worthy of praise. Now, seeking knowledge does not mean that you need to write a book or become an author. It means acquiring knowledge that will open doors for you and bring greater meaning to your life. You are in a small, dark room, and as you seek knowledge, candles will manifest all around you with blazing light, and the walls of the room will begin to expand. Soon, doors will become visible, each one leading to a hallway and further rooms. One day you will emerge victorious, with a higher status both in your inner world and your outer world. Knowledge makes the lowly grand, the weak strong, the ruled the ruler. Nothing compares to the power of knowledge, and you can have it if you decide to act today. I truly believe the pursuit of knowledge is the holiest of fields. The greatest favour you can do for yourself is to invest at least the time you are now wasting. For example, in a traffic jam, instead of listening to the antics of shock DJs, why not listen to audio books? You can finish an average of a book per week. This knowledge seeking will manifest in the form of material wealth. I guarantee it.

Self-elevation is the art of inner observation, which naturally expands your exterior world. Your life will begin to prosper internally and externally, without a doubt.

You must remember the following:

- Inner awakening begins with shedding light on the inner conversation between the opposing thoughts attached to every desire or decision for action.
- To unlock the gifts of the universe, you must prove that you are worthy of them.
- Worthiness is derived from a noble purpose and inner mastery.
- Miracles need action, action needs decisions, and decisions need positive thoughts.
- It is not enough to seek knowledge; you must engrave it within you. Only then you will be elevated.
- Remember the element of slow change. Do not rush into change but rather build it through one successful internal battle at a time.
- Master the knowledge of how to love. Learn how to love, and become love itself.

***

Fortify knowledge of the opposites
"If a man wants to be brave without first being merciful, generous without first being frugal, a leader without first wishing to follow, he is only courting death."
—Lao Tzu

In this partial quote from the *Tao Teh Ching* (translation by John C. H. Wu) shows three crucial elements that we need to learn: mercy, frugality, and following. It is only after we understand these principles that we can understand their opposites.

Why is sage-hood such an exalted status?

1. It requires mastery of the most difficult forces hijacking us inside.
2. It is a status of overcoming anger and allowing no emotions to master the intellect.
3. Most importantly, it is a state of controlling all opposing forces within.

This explanation demonstrates how one quality can be mastered and controlled only when its opposite quality is either mastered or controlled. I cannot know love if I haven't experience hate. Yet, I cannot truly love unless I am capable of controlling or diminishing my hate.

Likewise, being generous means understanding *frugality*. This involves knowing that frugality, when extreme, can lead to a stingy, strapped life. It is my opinion that generosity is the key to richness.

Omar Ibn Alkhattab, the second *khalifah* (the second ruler after Abu Bakr Al-Seddiq) was walking in the desert one day and heard that a revelation had descended upon prophet of Islam Muhammad (peace be upon him) asking the faithful to give from their wealth to the poor and for the sake of Allah. Omar smiled and said to himself, "Finally, now I can beat Abu Bakr Al-seddiq (the first ruler after the death of Prophet Muhammad) at something. These men competed in their faith by always trying to do more for the cause and to God. Omar very early in the morning took half of all his wealth and his family's wealth and rushed to deliver them for charity. Then he smiled, because Abu Bakr did not show up. However, he waited for him, assured that Abu Bakr would not hesitate in answering the call of Allah.

Finally, Abu Bakr appeared, and Omar rushed to him. "What brought you, Brother Abu Bakr?" he asked.

"What brought you brought me—to give in the sake of Allah and his messenger, peace be upon him." Abu Bakr replied, then he asked, "So, how much did you give, Brother Omar."

Omar replied with a smile, "Half of all that I own."

Abu Bakr said, "I am proud of you. May Allah reward you," and he kept on walking.

Omar said, "Brother Abu Bakr, how much did you give?"

"All my wealth," Abu Bakr replied, "and my family's wealth, Brother Omar."

Omar shook his head and smiled. "By Allah," he said, "no one can beat Abu Bakr on the path to Allah."

This story elevated Abu Bakr to a very high stature in the Islamic World. Generosity is highly valued in the Christian world as well, for Jesus said, **"If thou dost will to be perfect, go away, sell what thou hast, and give to the poor, and thou shall have treasure in heaven, and come, follow me" (Matthew 19:21).**

Remember that even qualities labelled as evil or undesirable are necessary survival instincts for you and me. Anger, for example, is needed to give you a sense of existence and for you to defend your mental, physical, and material territory. However, if anger becomes an autopilot system, it will lead to your ultimate misery and destruction. Relationships will suffer, abuse will ensue, you will attract hatred rather than love, and your life will endlessly dwell in a circle of autopilot-driven responses to external forces. Awakening is mastering the art of observing your entire inner field and the ability to hone these fields to coexist peacefully and productively with your external environment.

The last point in the quote at the top of this chapter speaks about the mastery of *following* in order to earn and succeed in the domain of leadership. Reflecting on this crucial point is to come to understand others. In order for you to assume a post that commands others, you must understand what lurks inside those who are commanded. Once you observe your feelings, inner thoughts, reactions, actions, and total experiential field in a position of following, you will be capable of predicting outcomes resulting from your leadership tactics in the future. Understanding the actions of others by experimenting through your own involvement in the role of the follower will help you emerge as a true leader.

Many ignore this rule, falling into the trap of "rushing to the top of the mountain." While in the lower ranks, many of us concentrate only on the role we seek to acquire. As we pass through all our feelings, reactions, and various mental and physical states as followers, we ignore the experience and consequently learn nothing. Our focus is to reach the top without observing the wise laws and rules to master our role once we reach it. Do you want ten million dollars? Allow me to ask you, would you even know how to handle this money? Can you assure me that it wouldn't lead to your ultimate demise? We arrive at the role of leadership through tenure, connections, by warming up to the boss or by sheer luck, and then we suffer and fail miserably. Why? I leave you to ponder the answer.

As humans we are composed of opposing inner fields and constantly subject to similar opposing external fields. These factors do not exist simply to cause our suffering but to force our learning. The path of least resistance is the one we follow by welcoming all that comes through the door of our material physical existence. We can then become masters, graduating as beings who can not only control and master our selves but also give valuable feedback to humanity as a whole. When you truly change from the inside, your change is reflected on the outside. Try it by changing and mastering one inner battle towards your higher self. For example, if you are dominated by the constant desire to talk, force yourself to remain completely silent at your next social gathering. Watch how everyone will think that there is something wrong with you. This indicates that change induces a reaction. While you are silent, observe those around you. Listen to what they say and observe their body language. Try to penetrate the meanings behind their words. Try to identify those on autopilot. It's an incredible experience. Through listening, you will gain greater understanding of your friends—their needs, aspirations, fears, and weaknesses. You can then use this knowledge to get closer to them or to help them. Try the exercise above as you embark on your internal battle towards a productive, positive decision. Go with it as far as you can go. With time, you will understand the great extent to which the inner self affects and shapes your outer world.

* * *

Chapter 10: The Mosquito

A few hundred years ago, a massive army gathered to conquer a weak nation. The leader of the conquering army was the most brutal and strong of warriors. He was also very arrogant and confident. He proclaimed that he would destroy the opposing army in a few hours. His opposition were truly scared, knowing they were about to perish, their women ravished and their children enslaved. Luckily for them, a mosquito plunged into the leader's skin, transmitting malaria into his bloodstream. The mighty warrior fell ill with fever and chills and died. His death led to the defeat of his mighty army. Can you imagine such a weak insect causing the defeat of such a mighty army? I leave you to contemplate this.

In the Quran, the book of the Muslims, a verse is worth bringing forth in Surah Albaqarah (The Cow) 2:26: "Indeed, Allah is not timid or shy to present an example—that of a mosquito or what is smaller than it or above it. And those who have believed know that it is the truth from their lord. But as for those who disbelieve, they say, 'what did Allah intend by this as an example?'"

Bringing attention upon as small a creature as an insect glorifies the important role of every object on our planet. Scientists have also revealed insects even smaller than mosquitoes that play a vital role in our ecosystems, which explains part of the verse above. Nothing is irrelevant, and all creatures deserve the respect of contemplation.

On daily basis, you must bring forth your awakened mind—the awareness of internal and external forces surrounding you. This concept can be applied to the smallest things. The next time you are rushing to find a parking space so you can meet up with friends at the movie theatre or the neighbourhood cafe, try to stop as soon as you park and reflect for a moment. Make a conscious decision to pause for just sixty seconds and bring your alert mind to the rampage of thoughts pushing you to park fast and get to the gathering fast. Take sixty seconds to breathe deeply and say to yourself, "I am awake and present and in control of my inner domain." *You* must decide when to come out of your car, not the forces behind rushing you.

Master what truly drives you

The desires you have inside you—for example, to enjoy the company of friends or the aroma of freshly brewed coffee—do not serve your true inner you. Your true inner self enjoys no coffee, tea, or snacks, and your attraction to your friends is in fact merely the ego reinforcing itself through a social network. This social network provides future favours and materialistic rewards. This does not mean you should never make connections, have fun, or satisfy your physical desires, but rather you must practice awakening and observing each action in relation to each part of your material existence. Love, sex, money, conversations, food and drink, work, fame, status, and friendship each serve part of your material existence. Your material existence begins to reach a higher altitude when all its needs are organized and purified under the leadership of your awakening and inner mastery.

When you practice inner leadership, your thoughts—particularly your inner beasts—are slowly tamed as time passes. You are with time no longer a prisoner to the hijacked mind. Every time you direct your attention inward, separating your source from all thoughts inside you and reclaiming who you truly are, a force inside you is strengthened—a force to observe and to direct your inner vessel. Often we fall to the trap of guilt, remorse, and self-blame when we engage in actions opposed to our natural, deeper source of peace. The hijacked mind often leads to a ruinous life, measured not only by lack of material possession but by lack of internal abundance.

I am not suggesting that you become a master of mastery, a path sought by few. Rather, I am suggesting mastering the balance needed to reclaim the chaotic inner domain that often governs your time-related existence. The life that surrounds you is nothing more than the sum of the decisions made and pursued by your hijacked self. The damage you currently see in your life—the guilt, remorse, pain (physical and emotional), financial scarcity, and wounded relationships—is the natural result of a sleeping mind, manifestations on the material plane that happened over time. It is powerful to accept that what has become took time to develop; it will take time to subside.

Often sages, wise men and women, try to convince us that it is possible in an instant to change and immediately reverse these powerfully gripping feelings and emotions; however, it is far wiser to reclaim your whole natural healthy inner self over time. Accepting the process of healing is a major step to ensuring an inner commitment.

The wisest celebration is the celebration of small successes along the path of recovery and awakening. Remember this the next time the phone rings; decide not to answer and choose not to be claimed by external forces. This does not mean that you should exist in a state of non-attachment to external or internal forces, but rather to switch off your autopilot self. You are in control, only you decide to engage or disengage. Even if you continue to live the way you have always lived, you must awaken to the fact that you are hijacked. This is the smallest form of awakening: admitting your hijacked state of existence but choosing not to do anything about it. You may not wish to turn off your autopilot state, but at least you are not completely oblivious to it, in a state of full sleep. Once you are able to master this process, knowing what truly motivates you to act in this world, you will become stronger in the face of your inner self, and you will decide when you will diminish the negative actions you indulged in throughout your existence. Slowly, you will become the director of your internal and external state, and healing will spread throughout your body, mind, and soul.

* * *

PART 3: PURIFY YOUR HEART

Chapter 11: Conditions of the Heart

Consider the many heart-related metaphors we use to describe our feelings: a broken heart, a bleeding heart, an aching heart, light/heavy hearted, a big heart, and so on. Have you ever asked yourself why we ascribe an organ composed of tissue with such a huge range of emotions? Scientifically speaking, we all know that the heart is composed of muscle tissue, mostly water. It is the pump that spreads blood throughout the body—so much each day that if you were to pump the same amount of blood by hand, you would be completely exhausted at the end of the day.

The heart is our one major feature that elevates us above the rest of the beasts that dwell on the earth. It is the pure place where the truth is hidden but available once you are able to polish off the rust accumulated after years of negligence and abuse.

The heart is where man came to know God, love, and his path. The body is simply the vehicle in which the inner heart travels towards its destination. With your body, you can sleep with someone for one night and walk away. With your heart, you can be with someone for fifty years.

A newborn has a glow in its face that is incredibly attractive to the loving eye. The way we react when we see a newborn is our heart jumping out to remind us of the source. The face glows with pure light, indicating peace inside. As we age, our faces collect the same dust we bring inside. We reflect what is in our heart. The eyes, the door to the inner kingdom, reveal the truth. The heart is the most sensitive of all, because it is purer than all.

The decisions you make throughout your life leave their impressions on your heart. Picture it as an empty vessel made out of the purest components, not of this world. As you age, you rent out this vessel to the most abusive of tenants. The pain you experience comes to a halt once you evict those saboteurs, and you begin to reclaim your source of purity as tenants of elevation, peace, and a noble cause take their place. The greatest enemy resides inside you.

There are three conditions of the inner self heart:

- The evil state
- The confused state
- The assured state

As you look inward at your heart, you will find yourself in one of these three states. The goal, the assured state, is a place of complete serenity, where you are fully aware of your source and confident in where you are going and ending. This is the state of the awakened and the true believers in the noble path. These individuals are generally unaffected by the "buzz" of the world. Unshaken by worldly events and wealth, they go about their day diligently and with patience. Awaiting the true journey back to the source, their life is about serving others, and they find pleasure in the simpler things in life. They are clear about their objectives. They can be multimillionaires (and many amongst them are), or they could be poor or middle class. It is all the same. Lack to them is a test and a chance for reflection and fewer material attachments. Abundance to them is about giving and spreading hope. Wealth expands their inner good and weakens their inner opposition. They have no resistance, and they are in a complete surrender to what they believe in. They are confident that what is meant for them will come, and what is not meant for them will never arrive. In either case, they are faithful in their work and put their heart in all they do. They are at peace, and their hearts are pure.

The heart is truly a miracle. If you will, please place your hand on the left side of your chest and take a moment to focus on the machine pumping within. Take sixty seconds before you continue reading. Realize the absolute greatness of this complex organ, ticking away at its constant rate. At the same time, reflect on how truly fragile you are. Yes, once this heart stops pumping, it is all over. The lights are out and the mission has come to its close, and the path will open to your great truth: What has made this organ pump for so many years? This exercise of placing your hand on your heart is my gift to you. It has helped me put things into prospective whenever my life became bleak, difficult, or simply unbearable. The very knowledge of how delicate life is, and how fragile our existence is, brings back a smile to my face.

I breathe deeply and realize what a marvellous gift it is just to be here, what an honour it is to be given the opportunity to experience and offer gratefulness and love, to do all that I can within the short time given to me. The time allotted to me is so precious that neither slumber nor obstacles shall stop me from enjoying every moment. I shall value the bad moments and the good, as long as I exist in the present moment.

I believe and know (despite the inability to prove it) that the heart is where your true inner consciousness lies. It is inside the heart that the source of the knowledge of the unknown originates. Even our intelligence resides in the heart, not in the brain. The brain serves as the mainframe computer—it stores information, directs traffic, sends signals, and produces orders that serve survival, motion, and reaction functions on the corporeal side—but the heart is where the decisions are made. The heart is our distinctiveness and our true character. While we are in a state of doing and being, all that we are is a result of our deeper origin, our source. It is there that who we are is true and real. Our physical existence is nothing more than the collector of credits, experiences, and traits, but the deep source, the heart, is the true observer and leader of the kingdom within and without. When you receive a trophy marking a success from your own heart, you will have reached the honourable garden.

Can you look at a child three days old and say he or she is evil? Can you say he or she is talkative, arrogant, proud, jealous, greedy, stubborn, sturdy, kind, giving, depressed, anxious, inhibited, or any of the traits and characteristics we see in adults? The answer is no, because a child represents our true inner soul and consciousness. As we age, we acquire environmental influences. Our earliest teachers are our parents and family members. It is through their presence that we acquire our autopilots and become the hijacked individuals we are today.

In the words of Bono, "Let freedom reign! Every village, every hamlet, every state, every city, let freedom reign!" The true freedom is the freedom of the inner heart—the return to the elemental place of the free self, for this is the true reason of this existence. Every step we take navigated by our autopilot-hijacked self is a step towards pain, sorrow, guilt, anxiousness, depression, conflict, instability, uneasiness, inner conflict, outer conflict, and chaos—and a step farther from God, in whatever form you recognize him.

Those symptoms mentioned above are nothing more than signals from your heart, screaming in your every atom, calling you to wake up and realign yourself with your true higher and noble you. Even those who have slipped completely into a state of autopilot and seem to be on a path of bliss must eventually come face to face with a hammer of catastrophic proportions. Suicide, murder, insanity, sudden disasters, and much more are the product of a deep void between the true inner self and the autopilot state. The pain of anxiety, fear, discomfort, imbalance, depression, frustration, anger, discontentment, and more are nothing more than the pain inflected by the ego-driven existence seeking the refuge of material wealth. It is not true that your ego is not you. That is a terrible way to withdraw from your responsibility. You created your ego, by allowing your surroundings to hijack you. Once you stand up and realize you have the power to overcome the inflated, painful, controlling ego, you can again become the master of your deeds and actions.

The ego is nothing more than a violent hijacking by your autopilot in violent pursuit of physical desires. It is a manifestation of your many inner conflicts. In the material side of our existence sits the bed of endless desires. I would never suggest that we all become Jesus figures, or non-combatants in a world that requires action and activities. We should all aspire to become achievers and create a life of harmonious, rich existence and fulfillment. In fact, I do not believe that it is ignoble to pursue dreams or achieve greatness. We all, individually, possess prominence once we awaken from the autopilot-hijacked state. I, and you, are worthy of achieving all we want to achieve, as long as we do it while we are in alignment with our higher self.

> *"The most incredible phenomenon is that those who are truly aligned and in a state of true inner tranquillity attract wealth, but with the least struggle and in a serene and effortless way. Why? Because they have awakened to the understanding that the awakened self is nothing less than the utmost service of others."* —LR

Perhaps you are in a state of self-blame. You experience guilt, doubt, agitation, discomfort, and dissatisfaction, running back and forth between the noble path and the crooked path. This is a lower state compared to the one described above, but at least this is a sign that you are in a state of inner struggle. Confused between materialism and spiritualism, you are clearly dissatisfied with the answers at hand. Anxious and unhappy as you travel down the path of pure materialism, you seek answers to complex questions, yet you lack the understanding of the spiritual inner path. You can be saved.

In this stage, you are similar to a heavy drunkard, unaware that he is completely out of control and running in the middle of the highway, like a madman. While he is running, he thinks he is in a state of bliss, but he is soon to face a rude awakening. This is the most difficult state in which to find awakening, as you are completely engulfed by your inner hijacked state. Even while you are reading this book, you may be completely oblivious and even contemplating tossing the book away. You cannot see beyond the physical aspect of your world and are immersed in your materialist beliefs. The only solution to your problem is a tailor-made personal disaster of heavy proportions to shake you into true awakening. The only awakening you seek involves ways to make more money. Believe me, I know. I am a veteran financial advisor.

Remember, thousands of rich, powerful men and women live a life of pain, anxiety, suicidal thoughts, loneliness, and complete inner chaos. Many even write books that attack anyone who attacks wealth as a source of despondency in order to defend their own lack of understanding. Money is armament in a malicious world, and money can make the external life extremely easy. While the rich do not worry about rent or bills, their autopilot self may still be on a mission of destruction, exploiting many other facets of their physical existence to take them as far away from their deep source of origin as possible, the place where purity resides. This is the test, the greatest battle many men and women face. Wealth can be the best tool the autopilot-hijacked self has at its disposal, destroying you when you least expect it. Does that mean that you should not build wealth? On the contrary, I am saying seek wealth while awake, and witness the glory of incredible expansion.

The steps to purification

Awakening to our inner self and reappointing ourselves to the Supreme Court of our internal existence will take us to our prominence. Greatness is a state of internal gratification and unwavering joy. It is your duty to purify your heart.

The purification of the heart is a three-step process:

1. Identify your ailments.
2. Understand the motives behind your ailments.
3. Erase your ailments.

Identifying your ailments is not a very complicated exercise. The identification process is one of *observation*. Observe how you react to and feel about news, events, incidents, and developments in the lives of those you know or hear about. Let's assume as you meet with a good friend on a Saturday afternoon and that he or she reveals that they have been promoted to a senior post at work, including a 20 percent raise. Notice your internal dialogue at this point. While you would surely congratulate him or her and express your happiness, keep your inner eye on your inner dialogue, feelings, and even physical reaction to the news. You probably will come to affirm an ailment if it exists. It could be jealousy or self-pity if you are not where you want to be financially. Regardless of the reactions manifesting inside you because of the news, notice that it outlines an ailment, likely the result of the autopilot reaction to hate reminders of the success of others. It also points towards another ailment, that of materialism, resulting in placing judgmental labels upon yourself and others.

Do you evaluate yourself and others based on their material possessions, appearances, the car they drive, the home they live in, or the partner they have? Notice if your appreciation of others is financially based or based on a reflection of your own existence. If you suffer from this affliction, you will be destined to live a life of pain, because you will always find someone whose material accomplishments are greater than yours, no matter where you are on the ladder of the material life. Many fall deeply into this trap, and their life simply becomes a nightmare, a constantly unfolding disaster of increasing misery.

The same is true when it comes to selecting your path partner—your husband or wife. Notice how you judge every female or male as they pass by you or meet you. Contemplate your inner evaluation of these people. Do you see beauty, or do you always notice the shortcomings of any physical appearance? Are you focused on what people say or on what fashion designer they are wearing? It is vital to understand that this materialistic evaluation method will result in a marriage filled with disasters. Your mind is clouded and poisoned by one evaluation method—physical attractiveness and sexual desire—so that all else vanish and appear only later, down the road, when you discover that your life has become a living nightmare and that you valued the wrong things in a partner.

Your autopilot self, driven towards the materialistic, made you ignore the fundamental factors for establishing a healthy relationship—intelligence, common ground, kindness, forgiveness, a subtle nature, or whatever criteria one sees as fit for a successful, genuine relationship. I have come to learn how unique and special each of us is. This does not mean to deny the strong foundation of physical desire attraction is based on. But it is a genuine encouragement to build a spiritual, mental, and noble relationship as strong as the physical pleasurable aspect can provide.

Understand that the motivation behind your ailment is simply your autopilot-hijacked self submitting to an inner desire. That's why sexual desires are so strong; it's why you see grownup, wise men get into car accidents because they can't keep their eyes on the road rather on a beautiful lady passing by. It was reported in the news recently that a five-car accident resulted from the sight of a beautiful female passing by. This is also the major reason behind so many destroyed relationships and failed marriages. While this book may have awakened you to the fact that you are in the wrong relationship, it does not mean you now have the excuse to cheat. You have the right to sever the relationship in a kind, calm manner only after you attempt to awaken your partner, who may be lost due to his or her own autopilot hijacking.

The pain resulting from the hijacked self can at times be extremely destructive. Every so-called grotesque person who indulges in horrific acts unacceptable to God and society is deeply hijacked by the powerful autopilot self, fuelled by uncontrollable desires that seek to dominate his or her complete existence. It is time for you to understand that these desires are not you but, dangerously, are traits rising out of your material existence. They seek only one goal: satisfaction.

The stomach, for example, is a unique organ that has two major tasks: send signals of emptiness and digest food. That is the function it was designed for, and so the stomach should seek only what it needs. But if you allow it to hijack you, it will seek larger and larger amounts of food, and more often. The miracle of your composition is that when you lose complete control and deliver your world to your stomach, your inner body eventually manifests this sabotage through ulcers, heart attacks, and fainting, sending you powerful messages to stop. The *food* did not cause the ulcers or the heart attack; your deep consciousness, your heart, caused it as a warning sign for you to retreat, wake up, and reclaim control. When the body dies an unnatural death, it is simply because your spiritual side, experiencing life through the physical side, gave up on your ability to steer your own ship and decided to go back to the non-physical world. God knows what he created and knows when you will go back. However, you always possess the choice to awaken and regain control to avoid such a sudden, pitiful demise. Do not throw yourself in the path of destruction, do not commit suicide, and do not kill are all orders from any religion that speaks of God.

When anyone intentionally breaks the law, for example, part of their current condition is uncovered. Drinking and driving, for example, signals a personality completely under the control of the autopilot self, which seeks to satisfy the desire of escaping from a painful, selfish existence. Further, it indicates a character that is not aligned with the noble purpose of serving others. By their actions behind the wheel, they endanger the precious lives of other people. This is a terrible state to be in. How do we fix that? Some suggest severe punishments, while I would suggest a six-month intensive course on humanity, sobriety, and the art of returning to a noble existence. While we need punishment for transgressors, we also need to address—collectively, as a society—the deeper problems the individual is facing in this day. Severe punishments can reduce or deter us from committing horrible actions, but they can never truly erase such actions, because one can respect the law for ten years and then break it in a horrific, catastrophic manner if they fall to despair. We must awaken to solving our failings and shortcoming at the deep source. We should start at the school level and at a young age.

Similarly, we must observe the mistakes we commit and the trespasses we indulge in and draw closer through this observation to a deeper understanding of what is winning the internal battle for our domination. Notice how this fits with my earlier call for freedom through the words of Bono. I understand that it is hard to break free from the hijacked self, but you are already on your way to healing and reclaiming who you truly are, by unveiling the inner composition of your existence. The very fact that you are beginning to observe your self is an astounding step towards self-control, restraint, elevation, and healing. This action will eventually become a habitual trait and an easy exercise to implement. It is you becoming your own best friend.

The exercise of thinking inwardly as opposed to outwardly gives you power and reward no amount of money can buy. You are enlightened, awake, and alert to your internal conversation, even when you are in a loud, lively party or gathering. With time, even the strongest stressors will bounce right off the strong, resilient new awakened you.

Imagine your boss summoning you into his office, then informing you that you are fired. Notice even as you imagine this how your inner self reacts. Are you shocked, disappointed, crushed, depressed, afraid, destroyed, or even speechless and surprised? Now imagine suddenly as you get this bad news that you actually *smile* and say to your boss, "Thank you for this opportunity. I knew I had to pursue who I truly am. Now I will have a few weeks to figure what I truly want to do with my life. This could be the long-awaited breakthrough to shake me out of this routine and this endless circle of nothingness. This could be the gate to an amazing new job or a chance finally to write that book I always dreamed of writing or to go after that business I wanted to build, convincing family friends and my local bank to help." Whichever way you react, you are still fired. The only difference is that if you truly look at it in the positive way described above, you will almost immediately erase the pain, the fear, and the confusion. Imagine walking out towards your favourite cafe and sitting down, saying,

- I have possibilities.
- I have the freedom to think.
- I am ready for what is next.
- I want more through the noble path.

Is your mind pumping positive or negative thoughts? Naturally it will pump negative destructive thoughts as a result of your materialistic autopilot side, which has been in control for so long. Now imagine your thoughts after performing the awakening exercises I have been speaking about. You are now in control of your inner self and the battles between your opposing thoughts. You realize that these thoughts do not represent you but simply represent their own desires and self interest. Yes, thoughts have self-interest—to exist and grow and stay—just like any organism.

Trees want to survive, animals want to survive, you want to survive, and your thoughts want to survive. Thoughts become inner beasts and absolutely destroy you while you are observing and thinking that everything is normal. Yes, I should be very angry about what my boss did. Yes, this child deserves to be beaten hard, and my wife deserves to be punished and slapped. Notice how all spouse abusers later on apologize, expressing remorse and sorrow. Their abusive trait is an autopilot hijacking, the result of feelings of inadequacy, jealousy, lack of self-esteem, dominance, anger, stress, the inability to communicate, and even substance abuse. When he comes back to apologize, his feelings of guilt, remorse, kindness, and shame can manifest because all those intense autopilot forces are now asleep. We all have opposing forces inside us, and all humans that experience anger, frustration, sorrow, despair, hate, love, and much more. It's up to us how we deal with our duality of inner feelings.

If we are not awakened, we will always live under the mercy of these forces and continue to live a catastrophic existence. Let the sun rise and warm you inside. This sun is the ability to illuminate your inner conversation and re-engage in directing your emotions and feelings. Thoughts shape our life because they trigger the autopilot-hijacked state, which orders your physical self to act in ways that will manifest the inner world's need to survive in an external environment. If your feelings and desires for food become a monster, the result will be obesity and health problems. If you're hijacked by sexual desires, you will end up breaking up a wonderful relationship, hurting others, or even attracting sexual transmitted diseases.

Like everything, even your endless pursuit of money and possessions can lead you to unethical, unacceptable, and even criminal activities, similar to the likes of Bernard Madof, who swindled investors out of fifty billion dollars. Can you imagine the enormity of spending forty years cheating so many people, including your closest family members? This is the pinnacle of the hijacked mind, running solely on autopilot without a moment's reflection. The result is obliteration and pain. People kill for money or love, but they also kill for far more pathetic reasons. Why would anyone kill another human being unless that person was fully hijacked by feelings and thoughts of inadequacy? I urge you to awaken, because you might not even be aware of where you are heading. Your life today is the summation of actions manifested to fulfill the desires of your autopilot-hijacked mind. Awake or perish and live a meaningless, painful life. You choose you decide.

No murderer, swindler, cheater, abuser, fanatic, or extremist ever woke up one day and said, "Ah, let me see, I want to become a murderer today." We become what we are heading to becoming as the result of the decisions we made while we were on autopilot. You could be reading this book sitting in your first-class plane seat, having just closed a major contract that will add millions to your bank account, not knowing that two years from now, you will go to jail for the rest of your life because you killed someone. Or perhaps you will become the next Bernard Madof, constantly ignoring the inner signals that what you are doing is wrong. You may smile and say, *are you talking about destiny?* My answer is that I am talking about your inner chaos leading to your ultimate demise.

> "Love yourself and be awake today, tomorrow, and always.
> First establish yourself in the way, then teach others, and so
> defeat sorrow."

—Adapted from the Dhammapada, translated by Thomas Byrom

* * *

The final step in purifying the heart is eliminating your ailments by understanding your own inadequacy and your judgement of yourself. When you focus on controlling your inner world, which produces your higher self, this in turn develops your goals and personal aspiration, in line with who you really are and how you view yourself. As a master in the making, you begin to command feelings of non-envy to overcome those of envy, because you understand now that the accomplishments of one man do not undermine those of another (unless they are evil) and that your own shining moment is on its way. Better still, your shining moment can be one between you and yourself and not for the world to see, judge, or evaluate. You can be a king, a queen, a prince, a princess, or simply a whole person, by knowing that you are now a master and a sage, unshaken by the externalities of the world.

You will one day pass along and leave this world, and you will not care about what people have said and what you left behind, as long as along that journey you have been able to do two things:

1. Master your inner world, reflected in your external environment.
2. Give others all you can give to improve their lives and enhance their existence.

Perhaps you will accomplish this by sending positive messages to others with your pleasing appearance (smiling helps). Perhaps it is feeding one hungry man or helping a woman rise above an abusive relationship without expecting anything in return. Even for a more deeply materialistic

Westerner, you can pursue material wealth as long as you do it while amassing your higher self.

**

Love is the answer

The answer to the ascending process is LOVE. You must learn to love yourself and to love others. You must switch your inner feelings to the notion of giving, aiding, and loving. Love creates forgiveness, for others and for yourself. Love can diminish evil. When you love your friend, you won't speak ill of him when he is not around. When you love your parents, you will continue to visit them as they grow old. When you love your children, they will come to your aid when you are older. When you love your neighbour, you won't hurt his family or abuse his wife. When you love your work, you will serve others with the utmost respect and the highest level of morality. When you love yourself, you will then forgive yourself and bring forth a smile to others. Love is the foundation of a progressive, healthy life. Love can make you kinder, more agile and resilient, more understanding, and more human. The answer to purifying your heart is to love as much as you can, and to give as much as you can, and to fear god as much as you can.

Purifying your heart is to detach it from the material and attach it to the eternal. Substitute the love of money with the love of *life*, seeing each day as a blank sheet of paper waiting to be filled with good deeds. To have a pure heart is to cease to be envious or hating. It is to wish unto others as you wish unto yourself. It is to believe in abundance and eliminate thinking based on scarcity. Purifying the heart is erasing arrogance and greed and mastering asceticism. Purifying your heart is the process of understanding your weakness and your greatness at the same time. To witness the miracle you are is to be grateful for the opportunity to be, to love, to give, to help, to forgive, to seek beauty, and to reflect on the path towards the ultimate source.

Purifying your heart is to utter no hurtful words and *think* no hurtful worlds. This is not a utopia but a mission. While you are achieving all you want to achieve, you must do it while you are purifying your heart. What will millions do for you if you look in the mirror and have no respect for the man or woman you see? What will fame do for you if you are lonely among the masses? What will the great company you built mean if built on the ruins of the lives of others? The path to purifying your heart may seem difficult and long and in need of patience, but it is the only path that will cure you from the deepest illnesses of pain, anxiety, depression, fear, and self-hate.

Self-hate the tyranny of the mind

I felt compelled to write about a subject often denied by many but in fact shared by the masses. Self-hate is an integral component of man's mental makeup. Self-hate is often confused with an illness, or a form of punishment inflicted by the mind due to one's dissatisfaction with oneself and the lack of confidence one may suffer due to one's perceived lack of value in comparison to the world around him.

I will argue the contrary and reveal a secret that will change your life. Self-hate is in fact a *gift*, deeply planted in your subconscious and ready to manifest at any moment to keep you from straying from your true purpose. It is an alarm to your inner world that you are using false tools to evaluate yourself.

Why would anyone hate him or herself? The answer to this question varies from one person to another, but in general, self-hate falls under one of the following categories:

- Feelings of ugliness in comparison to others
- Feelings of inadequacy in the presence or knowledge of successful people
- Sinful or immoral acts committed by the self-hater
- Lack of purpose and objective in life
- Deep emotional dependency on people (particularly of the other sex)
- Inner ugly thoughts that keep popping up scaring you; obsessive compulsive behaviour (OCD)
- Lacking of certain gifts you wish to posses
- Constantly disappointing those around you/not living up to their expectations
- Believing the criticism and belittling of others

I call self-hate a *gift* because the self-hater is in a position of weakness. When you are weak internally, you need to be awakened to that fact, and sometimes this requires a powerful alarm. Hence, self-hate manifests, demanding action to restore the equilibrium of healthy existence. You see, everything depends on what you think of it. How you view a certain state of your mind is what *determines* your state of mind. Confused! Do not despair. It will soon become clearer.

Imagine life without inner alarms. Imagine life without a moral code. Imagine life without feedback from others. Imagine life without a single human around you. Would you have any feelings of self-hate then? The answer is most definitely no, because in such a world, there would be no moral code to follow, no people to transgress against or compare yourself to, and no desire to ascend higher on the ladder of success or whatever you believe shall give you value.

When you experience self-hate, you must enter a state of meditation that I call the "separation state." In this state, you must try to separate yourself from yourself and become an external observer of your complete condition. This means evaluating your physical appearance, your actions, and your inner emotional state. When you come to a global macro view of the personality before you, you can now begin the evaluation process.

Why does the person you just evaluated hate him or herself? Well, you might say things like, "He is overweight compared to others, and he has a sloppy appearance." Perhaps you found out "He hates himself for cheating on his spouse and ruining his marriage," or "He has purposely hurt a colleague by talking ill behind his back, resulting in him being fired." As you delve deeper, you notice that he hates himself because his parents always told him that he was a disappointment. Further into your observation, you discovered a state of deep envy of others and a deep desire to have what others have.

Once you have observed the reason behind the self-hate your subject experiences, you can begin the healing process. Write down all of the above on a piece of paper as follows:

1. Overweight
2. Sloppy appearance

3. Cheater and disloyal
4. Gossiping
5. No encouraging environment
6. Envy

After your analysis, you are ready for the next step, the *acceptance* phase. In this phase you will recognize that what's done is done, but you still carry a responsibility to seek reconciliation with it. What I am about to say might shock you, and you may reject it, but it is the only way you can move past acts of transgression and hurtful deeds against others.

You must approach the colleague you got fired, preferably over the phone, and you must muster the courage to do so regardless of the outcome. Remember that you are seeking to heal your inner mind from the mistake you have committed. When you call, you will confess, apologize, and seek forgiveness. This is not easy, but once it is done, a heavy cloud will be lifted from above you, and you will end the conversation by stating your willingness to help him or her in any way possible. If your colleague refuses to forgive you, abuses you over the phone, and insults you, you and your victim will have become equals in a way, and you will be released from the guilt. If there is anything left to repay, God will take care of it (and he *will* take it from you eventually). However, at this stage, you must move on.

The same principle applies if you rightfully owe someone money, even if your debt extends years back. I remember while in Charlotte North Carolina during my university days, the year the war in Kuwait took place and the money stopped coming from my parents. A friend passed me an envelope that had three hundred dollars inside. It was a big help in the interim, until I was able to sell my car and find a job.

The days passed, and I had to join my family in Canada. The connection between me and my friend was severed, as he went back to his homeland and I pursued my life in this new land. For exactly eighteen years I have pursued him and tried to locate him. I knew he was in Dubai, and I knew his name. I repeatedly failed to locate him. Eighteen years later at a hotel in downtown Dubai, I saw a group gathered, laughing and talking and having a great time. As I passed them by, I uttered greetings and one of the men in the group replied and extended his hand. In turn, I paused and shook his hand in return. He was a local, and I expressed my love for the city and the kindness of the people in Dubai.

It was a nice conversation, and just then it passed my mind to ask about my long-sought-after friend. So I asked him, "Do you know so and so?" And he smiled and asked me to hold a minute. He reached for his mobile phone on the table, dialled a number, and began speaking to someone on the other line. He told him "someone here wants to talk to you". I was in shock, thinking this was a joke. I took the phone and began by stating who I was, and behold, the man turned to be my long-sought friend.

We arranged to meet next day at Mina Salam, a luxurious hotel in downtown Dubai, and we met with screams and hugs. Eighteen years later, through a complete coincidence, I was able to offer my friend his money back, which he naturally refused. I was free from that shackle.

In the situation above, I was able to repay my debt relatively painlessly. If, on the other hand, your debt is large or you are unable to repay it, then do not run away, but try to come to acceptable terms. You will be astonished at people's generosity if you humbly state your abilities. On the other hand, there are those who are blinded by money and cannot see the condition of others, and that is their problem. What matters is doing what you can to alleviate the inner heaviness and to exercise morality correctly.

The second point to tackle is the immorality of cheating. Cheating on a spouse is, in my own humble opinion, the most horrific act a man or woman can commit. Both the married spouse and the outside man or women, pursuing this married spouse are equally guilty and truly despicable. This may strike you as harsh, but harshness is needed in this particular situation. The reason is that this one act truly diminishes and hurts others around you. We are all susceptible to the trap of this desire. Sexual desires are so strong that many honourable personalities have been destroyed by it and many homes have been destroyed. Once it has happened and is in the open, what is the solution? And the answer is never simple or straightforward. This is an act that cannot be taken back or corrected. It requires a huge sum of self-forgiveness and the forgiveness of those hurt by it. This is the time to resort to what is called your "circle of influence" referred to by Coach Dan Sullivan. The circle of influence is the place you can control or influence. You must apologize to your spouse and truly ask for his or her forgiveness. You must also be true to yourself if you deeply have no desire for the relationship to end it civilly, and you must exercise repentance deeply at the root.

Deciding not to indulge in such an error again should not simply be an utterance of words; it must go deeper than that. You must have an honest conversation with yourself regarding the true reason for committing such a crime. Once you know why you have done it, you can begin the inner healing needed. Remember that in marriage, you always have the choice of leaving or ending the relationship, but you have no right to stray. Many examine the reasons behind spousal affairs, and they offer great help on the subject. However, you must remember that reasons do not warrant the action.

After you receive the forgiveness of your spouse and children (if they knew about it), you must seek forgiveness from the power you believe in and dig deeper to forgive yourself. Hating yourself here is a clear, constant alarm that you are straying from the righteous path or the moral human code. Turn it into positive deeds and extend true love to your next spouse. Appreciate what you have and focus on building, not destroying. Whatever is out of your circle of influence is just not worth worrying about.

Appearance and weight happen to be one of the major instigators of self-hate. Now is the time to re-evaluate your standards and the standards of humans, not the million-dollar fake personalities projects depicted on TV. If you hate yourself because you do not look like an actress or an actor, then you are allowing the world to tell you how you should look. If you relate your weight to your health, then that is a valuable measurement. I have a funny theory about weight. I believe that weight is the penalty for the pleasure we receive from food and whenever I gain weight (and I do often), I simply accept it, because I want the pleasure of food. However, I always re-engage again in a plan to shed the extra weight and restore my body to a healthy form. I increase my water intake, I take supplements, I exercise, and I practice healthy eating.

The motivation of an actress could not be the same as that of an average individual. The compensation of millions of dollars and the availability of professional help 24/7 toward achieving their goal is far greater than the motivation to slip into an old pair of pants or to impress a few people around you. Allow yourself some slack, but whenever you wish to stop being fat, just stop eating too much and get up and join a gym. All other gimmicks are designed to curb your large appetite but cannot help you achieve the lifelong constant of perfect weight. In any diet, you must possess the desire to look better and be healthier, but far more important is the *will* to act. Add up all the positives you would receive from a thin figure on a piece of paper, and subtract the pleasures of overeating; only then will you begin to act. However, cut yourself some slack and enjoy life.

* * *

The final point I wish to tackle is emotional dependence on others. This is a problem you have faced since a young age at home. It is partly the fault of the parents; even without ill intentions, this happens to everyone. You must understand that others cannot make you happy if you do not know how to make yourself happy. When you lack the power to control your inner response to thoughts arising from the abuse of others, you will continue to suffer.

If you feel better about yourself only when your spouse says that you are smart, strong, or beautiful, then you have become a prisoner to your spouse and anybody who is willing to feed your ego. This is a huge disaster that eventually results in low self-esteem, lack of confidence, acceptance of abuse, broken relationships, and affairs.

In any study of the art of seduction, you learn that in order to seduce your prey, you must understand what they seek and what they lack. Once you possess that knowledge, your objective becomes achievable 90 percent of the time. If you wish never to be prey to the intentions of others, then you must establish a stronger inner source of self-evaluation and appreciation.

This does not suggest that we can fully disengage from our basic needs for appreciation, praise, encouragement, and feelings of being wanted, but we all must reduce our dependence and increasing our self-knowledge. By awakening from within, you can become your own inner master and the controller of your emotions. This will make you stronger. The *how* is in the way you think. I can tell you that you are beautiful, which should make you happy, but if I don't, it does not mean that you are not. If my opinion is not expressed, you must know that you are beautiful; my silence should not indicate otherwise.

A lack of praise does not mean you are not worthy of praise, and the utterance of disappointment by others does not mean that you are a disappointment. You are a human on a learning curve. Allow yourself room to grow and improve. We are all sinners; we are all weak at times, and none of us are perfect. We do, however, seek to become higher and better human beings. If this *will* exists, then the pursuit is noble and the results will surely come.

Remember to flip negative inner feeling into positive indicators of your swayed position from the balanced core.

Anxiety, depression, lack of confidence, and low self-esteem, and other forms of self-hate are always the result of:

- Lack of knowledge
- Ill deeds
- Shifting from the righteous path and the higher self to the crocked path and the lower self

Every condition inside you is a cry for some sort of correction. These can be summarized as follows:

- Stop seeking strength from others and seek strength from within.
- Change your habits through action not wishing.
- Eliminate harmful dependencies such as alcohol, drugs, and overeating even if it means seeking professional help.
- Stop desiring what you don't have and just focus on what you have and what you can do to improve your condition building on what you have.
- Stop thinking that the size of your pocketbook is who you are.
- Seek knowledge and wisdom.
- Stop what is immoral and increase what is moral. This can be improved if you choose better friends.
- Learn to appreciate the power of patience.
- Believe that the eternity of the present is a myth. Things change all the time.
- Be open to the world and what is coming.
- Be positive, hopeful, and appreciative.
- Listen! Love will always knock on your door if you are willing to listen.

- Make sure you get up to open the door when opportunity knocks.
- Health is your priority. If you are disabled, search for ways to compensate. We all have skills and abilities.
- When you seek a purpose, always make it as worship—noble and useful.
- Learn the power of the moment and what you are experiencing now, for it will surely pass, and so shall the next minute.
- Stop your obsessions and repetitive thoughts do not make them real.
- Learn to pay attention to your body by seeking idle hours, and hours to re-sharpen the saw.
- Hope is the flower in need of watering desperately by all of us.
- Life is truly short if you always seek happiness in some distant point in the future.

* * *

THE 20 SYRUPS OF REFLECTION

Certain statements can change your life, remove your inhibitions, open your eyes, move you, challenge you, motivate you, strike you with a blow to the head, teach you, aid you, and guide you. Meanwhile, other statements just pass you by.

I wanted to end this book with twenty statements that can do some of the above. Thinking is a gift if well focused and well directed. Never underestimate the power of a single thought if you believe in the thought wholeheartedly.

Throughout my life, I have made it a routine to choose one concept, one statement of wisdom, or one logical thought and use it over and over again. The simplest one is the concept of "So what," which has helped me tremendously in overcoming difficulties, especially when I was certain that I would need much patience before circumstances changed. Another statement I carry with me is "There is no time left" or "Time is running out," and this has truly revolutionized my life. Why? Because by telling myself this over and over again, motivation surges through my body to complete unfinished business and do what I was meant to do. Heeding this statement while erasing the fire of desire, I have been able to accomplish numerous projects small and big without pain. Even when you fail, you can invest this failure in future reflection, observation, and reconstructing.

Another concept that gives me tremendous help is "Surrender to a higher power." In the early stages of my life, I was not as concerned with this concept; my strength, aspiration, and hopes were all I needed. But when complex problems began to manifest in my life, when I met with resistance and my suffering began, my higher power, my creator, gave me solace.

This is not a call to convert to any particular religion, but I do believe that it is necessary to surrender to a force greater than yourself and beyond this world. A great danger is misunderstanding this concept and placing your worship in *material things*. If you do this, you will be destroyed and paralyzed if a spouse leaves you. If you lose your money, you will be devastated, broken, and perhaps devoid of any will to build again. These feelings are a result of worshipping things that will eventually leave you (or that you will leave when you die).

The bottom line is, if you do not surrender to a higher power, you are bound to suffer. You cannot even believe in your country, ultimately, for you often see corruption, greed, and hypocrisy in the public sector—and in this recent economical meltdown, you have certainly learned that within institutions that appear to be safe and trustworthy, thieves lurk in the dark.

For me, "Time is running out," "So what," and "Surrender to a higher power" are the ingredients for a happy life, for they combine alertness, motivation, solace, and the seed of action.

I will leave you now with twenty statements for you to think deeply about. If you do, I believe you will discover that they possess the ingredients for a truly powerful life.

1. "When we think we progress, but when we obsess we digress, so learn the difference." (LR)
2. "Life's trials and tribulations are nothing more than a mirage thought true by those who failed." (LR)

3. "It is not what you feel about a problem but how you choose to feel about the problem." (LR)
4. "Do for God as if you will die tomorrow and do for life as if you will live forever." (Ali Ibn Abe Taleb)
5. "The more you express yourself, the more trouble you create." (LR)
6. "Purifying the heart and the intention is harder than all other actions for those who truly act." (Ayoub As-Sakhtiyane)
7. "Long before Christianity, mankind believed in a life after death and therefore had no need of the Easter event as a guarantee of immortality." (C. G. Jung)
8. "It is, unfortunately, only too clear that if the individual is not truly regenerated in spirit, society cannot be either, for society is the sum total of individuals in need of redemption." (C. G. Jung)
9. "Learn and seek knowledge, for indeed none of you knows when he will be needed by the people." (Abdullah Ibn Masood)
10. "My sons seek knowledge. Scholarship makes the lowly noble, gives fame to the obscure, and raises slaves above emperors." (Ibn Abbas)
11. "For God commanded, saying, honour thy father and mother." (Jesus)
12. "Say, 'Indeed, my Lord extends provisions for whom He wills and restricts [it], but most of the people do not know.'" (The Quran)
13. "Every act of transgression shall visit you back unless you express sorrow and cease to transgress again." (LR)

14. "Those you look down on are grand in the eyes of their loved ones and grand in the sight of God." (LR)
15. "All desires, wants, and goals are a source of pain." (LR)
16. "A thousand friends to a person are not a lot, but one enemy is way too many." (Imam Shaafi'ee)
17. "Whoever seeks and searches for the mistakes and shortcomings of his fellow man is left with no friends." (Ash Shabi)
18. "When your brother (friend) is out of sight, speak about him in a way that you would want him to speak about you when you are out of sight." (Sufyan At-thawri)
19. "Do not wait to be humbled by the days and trials. Begin now" (LR)
20. "Seek a noble goal without the gathered pain and lose with a smile." (LR)

Conclusion

Every day that passes you by holds the memory of your deeds and the seeds of your actions. If you awaken the next day, you will have a new chance to become a better human being. This opportunity is no longer available to those who passed away in the night. This thought can be a strong motivator to commit to better action. Pain subsides and departs your body and mind with every step towards the higher you. We overvalue life and its events and therefore forget our awaiting hour of departure.

A man called Al-mazni visited a great scholar in the east called Imam Al Shaafi'ee during his departing moments on earth. Al-mazni asked Imam Shasfi'ee, "How have you awakened today my friend?"

Imam Shaafi'ee replied, "I have awakened from this life departing, from my family separating, from my friends leaving, from the glass of death drinking, and before my God standing, and I know not if my soul shall enter heaven; therefore I would congratulate it, or entering hell, therefore I would weep it".

We are all heading to one absolute event, the event of death. This should never depress us or even instil fear in our hearts. It is a blessing in disguise to be on this land no more after the end of the journey. It is one of my greatest motivating factors to do more, to build more, to give more, to love more, to care more, and to climb the ladder to the more noble me. This makes me value every moment and helps me indulge in the now, this moment. Obsessing about tomorrow or next week or in the distant future offers nothing more than misery at best. While we must plan and prepare, we must never lose sight of the most important thing above all, and that is to be alive in joy now.

The path of cleansing your inner world by shutting off old autopilots that have hijacked you for so many years is a noble and rewarding one. Observing yourself daily and measuring the progress of your inner awakening is a blissful experience. Do not be fooled by the mirage of difficulties and the presence of obstacles, for they too shall pass, and you shall meet new challenges and ride new curves along the way. The strength that emanates from inside is the strength you must seek for as long as you live. Allow not the days to shake you, break you, or erase you from within. You hold the gift of life in your hands and are capable of rising above the agony of daily living into the bliss of the centred self, the higher self, and the happy self.

I leave you now, but I will never forget you in my prayers, as I wish you will never forget me in yours. I ask God to bless you with a strong heart, an awakened self, a higher self.

AMEN

Author Bio

Loay is one of Canada's top emerging spiritual & motivational speakers. His 15 years experience as one of Canada's top financial & investment advisors helped him pave the way to understanding the human condition. Winner of the T.O.P award in management at Investors Group, and the number one producer at IGSI the year it was launched. He received his Bachelor of Commerce in International Business in 1994 from Concordia University in Montreal, and his Professional Financial Planner designation from IQPF in Montreal. Loay has received numerous awards in sales and considered a deep soul by many listeners to his speeches and message. Loay created a number of successful teams and lead the pact in training and inspiring. Loay speaks two languages fluently and can shake an audience constantly to reflect, observe, and change. His personal turmoil while earning over $400,000/year at age 29, paved the way for the emergence of a new dynamic deeply wise personality. Amongst his occupations, Associate Regional Director (Investors Group), Branch Manager (GMII), Agency Director (GMIS), Director and Founder (UPAM), and VP Elite Wealth Management (Monarch Wealth). Loay resides in Mississauga, Canada, and father for one son, Fadel.

Loay can be reached via email: **higheryou@gmail.com**

Made in the USA